CONVERSATIONS ON PHILANTHROPY

An Interdisciplinary Series
of Reflections and Research

Volume I
Conceptual Foundations

Lenore T. Ealy

SERIES EDITOR

® *DonorsTrust*
2004

Conversations on Philanthropy

Volume I, Conceptual Foundations

©2004 DonorsTrust

For information, address the business office:
DonorsTrust
111 North Henry Street
Alexandria, VA 22314

ISSN 1552-9592
ISBN 0-9761904-0-0

CONTENTS

Introduction

INTRODUCTION

This inaugural volume of *Conversations on Philanthropy: An Interdisciplinary Series of Reflections and Research* is titled "Conceptual Foundations," but it could have as easily been called "Reclaiming the Public." Our authors were asked to reflect on the state of contemporary economics and political philosophy and to consider what foundations these disciplines might provide in launching a series of conversations about the role of philanthropy in a free society.

What emerged from these considerations is an intriguing riff on the ambiguities of the term "public." Our authors variously speak of *public goods, public virtues,* and *public values* and the ways that they can be provided, cultivated, and made manifest. What is clear from these layerings of the term "public" is that the term itself has either outlived its analytical usefulness or is pregnant with a new meaning that needs yet to be born.

Philanthropy, to put a slight twist on its meaning, refers to love of the public, of humankind. Yet the public policy of the twentieth century welfare states went a long way in theory toward crowding out any meaningful work for voluntary philanthropy to accomplish. In the paradigm that emerged during the Progressive era, the role of republicans, patrons of the *res publica*, was largely to pay taxes and to support the administration of public health, education, and welfare by centralized bureaucracies of professional civil servants. Amateur philanthropists, those lovers of charity as both a substantive end of human action and an effective means of serving the public interest through private action, were overshadowed by a "scientific philanthropy" that sought to express love for mankind by sponsoring demonstration projects that might justify public funding and administration of uniform and "scalable" social welfare programs.

The result is a state of affairs in which the voluntary sector, once dreamed of as a truly independent domain by Richard Cornuelle (*Reclaiming the American Dream*, 1965), is now conceived of as a cog in the vast machinery of a system of "third-party governance." The term is that of Lester Salamon, who suggests that there is nothing unusual in the fact that nonprofit organizations are today heavily funded by governments, and who suggests that this is in fact a normative state of affairs that addresses the institutional problem of what he calls *voluntary failure*.

In *Conversation I* in this volume, Peter Boettke and David Prychitko, two leading economists of the Austrian school, serve up an initial critique of Salamon's paradigm of third-party governance and the notion of voluntary failure on which it is based. They explore how the Austrian tradition of economics, building on the work of Ludwig von Mises, Freidrich Hayek, Israel Kirzner, and others, might offer a more robust theory of not-for-profit and nonprofit decision making and a case for decoupling these voluntary organizations from government funding and oversight. Zoltan Acs, Emily Chamlee-Wright, Roger Lohmann, and Richard Stroup pick up the questions raised by Boettke and Prychitko and help give direction to what we intend here: not an *obiter dicta* conceptual solution but the beginnings of a conversation that we hope many of you will continue in your own communities.

Conversation II turns to an examination of the contributions that contemporary political philosophy might offer to our reflections on philanthropy. Steven Ealy's essay considers why a search for political solutions to social problems has become the default approach in America. Ealy examines the political philosophy of Leo Strauss and the political journalism of George Will—both typically considered "conservative"—and discerns in them an elevation of the political sphere as the superior domain of public life and the site of hegemonic authority over all other forms of both private and communal action. Ealy finds in Will's argument for "statecraft as soulcraft" haunting echoes of both classical political philosophy and Progressivism, and a stumbling block to the flourishing of a genuinely voluntary philanthropic sector composed of "independent institutions from which alternative visions of the good life could flow and which could legitimately participate in the public life of the community as a proponent of those views."

In the final section of his paper, Ealy suggests how the writings of Michael Polanyi and Michael Oakeshott point us toward more robust foundations for conceiving of philanthropic action and institutions as both sources of authority in their own spheres and creative participants in the working out of modern public life.

Eugene Miller, Gus diZerega, and Gordon Lloyd take up Ealy's questions and, while largely sympathetic to Ealy's effort to provide more solid ground for the legitimacy of philanthropic enterprise, seek to retain a constructive role for classical political philosophy in the working out of the problems of modernity. DiZerega, for instance, reintroduces us to Aristotle as a helpful contributor to modern political thought and action. In the end, however, each of our commentors in essence finds a need to recast the question as an inquiry into the nature of public action itself, revealing that further conversation is needed to liquidate the meaning of this ubiquitous and important but polyvalent term.

In an interesting twist on our question about the role of philanthropy in a free society, Miller also suggests the theme for our cover art. He recounts the tragedy of Prometheus, who stole fire from the gods of Olympus and gave it to mankind because of his *philanthropia*, his love for mankind. Miller enjoins us to reckon with the fact that Prometheus' well-intended act for the public good was accompanied by a disregard for the order of things and a pride in his own godlike knowledge of what was best for mankind. The story serves to remind us that private actors may be as likely as government bureaus to act on ill-informed motives or to neglect the unintended consequences of their beneficence, and that any private or government action taken for something as abstract as the public good is fraught with dangers. This observation warrants that we undertake deeper and more transparent conversations in public spaces about the ways and means by which people work together to achieve shared purposes.

Jazz music, with its unique blend of tradition and improvisation, has been called "the purest expression of American democracy; a music built on individualism and compromise, independence, and cooperation" (www.pbs.org). It is arguable that America's philanthropic tradition shares these cultural tensions and likewise makes a unique and important contribution to human life. It is our hope that by undertaking these conversations on philanthropy and its role in a free society we will come to a better understanding of the delicate balances between our individualism and our love of our communities, between our independence and our habits of cooperation, between our private and public roles. And not only to contemplate but to play our roles as better-informed participants, aware of the need for both the humility to respect and learn from our best traditions and the confidence to improvise and improve upon our life together.

— Lenore T. Ealy
Series Editor

CONVERSATION 1

Is an Independent Nonprofit Sector Prone to Failure?
Toward an Austrian School Interpretation of
Nonprofit and Voluntary Action

Peter J. Boettke and David L. Prychitko

WITH COMMENTS BY

Zoltan J. Acs

Emily Chamlee-Wright

Roger Lohmann

Richard Stroup

Conversations on Philanthropy Volume I: Conceptual Foundations

®DonorsTrust
2004

CONTRIBUTORS

ZOLTAN J. ACS is the Doris and McCurdy Distinguished Professor of Entrepreneurship at the University of Baltimore. His research interests include the role of entrepreneurship in innovation, economic development and social and historical development. He is the author of twenty books including *Entrepreneurship, Geography and American Economic Growth*, Cambridge University Press 2005, and *Entrepreneurship and Philanthropy in American Capitalism, Small Business Economics*. He is the recipient of the Swedish award for Research on Small Business and Entrepreneurship in 2000, and the editor of *Small Business Economics*.

PETER J. BOETTKE is Professor of Economics at George Mason University, where he is also the Director of Graduate Studies and a Senior Research Fellow at the Mercatus Center. Boettke is the editor of the *Review of Austrian Economics*. He is also the author of numerous articles in the professional journals and has authored several books, including *The Political Economy of Soviet Socialism, Why Perestroika Failed*, and *Calculation and Coordination*.

EMILY CHAMLEE-WRIGHT is Associate Professor of Economics at Beloit College. She is author of *The Cultural Foundations of Economic Development* (Routledge 1997) and co-author of *Culture and Enterprise: The Development, Representation, and Morality of Business* (Routledge 2000) with Don Lavoie.

ROGER A. LOHMANN is Professor of Social Work and Benedum Distinguished Scholar at West Virginia University and the Editor of *Nonprofit Management and Leadership*. He is the author of numerous journal articles, and author of three books: *Breaking Even: Financial Management in Human Services; The Commons: New Perspectives on Nonprofit Organization, Voluntary Action and Philanthropy; Social Administration* (co-authored with Nancy Lohmann) and co-editor (also with Nancy Lohmann) of *Rural Social Work Practice*. He is the founder and operator of ARNOVA-L, CGAP-L, and 20 other electronic discussion lists. He is currently involved in creating a research and training center focused on sustained dialogue, public deliberation and other approaches to public talk.

DAVID L. PRYCHITKO is a professor of economics at Northern Michigan University and faculty affiliate in the Program on Markets and Institutions of the James M. Buchanan Center for Political Economy. Formerly a visiting fellow in the Program on Participation and Labor-Managed Systems at Cornell University, and Fulbright fellow at the University of Zagreb, he was most recently awarded the Green Honors Chair in Economics at Texas Christian University for 2003-2004. Prychitko has published widely in economics, and is the co-author (with Paul Heyne and Peter Boettke) of *The Economic Way of Thinking*, an introductory textbook published by Prentice Hall.

RICHARD STROUP is professor of economics and interim department head at Montana State University and a senior associate of the Property and Environment Research Center (PERC). During the Reagan administration, Stroup served as the director of the Office of Policy Analysis at the Department of Interior. He is a widely published author and speaker on economics, including natural resources and environmental issues. His books include the recent primer on economics, *Eco-Nomics: What Everyone Should Know About Economics and the Environment*, and a leading economics principles textbook, co-authored with James D. Gwartney, *Economics: Private and Public Choice*, now in its tenth edition.

Is an Independent Nonprofit Sector

Prone to Failure?

Toward an Austrian School Interpretation

of Nonprofit and Voluntary Action

Peter J. Boettke and David L. Prychitko

Introduction

Nonprofit organizations have traditionally been considered a legitimate alternative source for the services provided today primarily by the bureaucratic welfare state (Berger, Neuhaus, and Novak, 1996). Taken together, nonprofit organizations can be viewed as a vibrant but largely "independent" sector characterized by a spontaneous ordering of associations that are founded neither on the state's compulsory power nor on the capitalist's search for private monetary profit (Cornuelle, 1965). In an extensive body of work, however, Lester Salamon, one of the leading scholarly investigators of nonprofit organizations, questions the "independence" of the sector.[1] Salamon argues that the U.S. has a long, established history of efficient institutional linkages between the nonprofit sector, which he calls the "voluntary sector," and the state. Rather than a substitute or alternative source of services, Salamon sees nonprofits as being in an effective "partnership" with the state, a viable form of "third-party" governance. He argues that the independent sector is, in fact, not so independent, and that on its own it is prone to failure. Salamon points to the aftermath of the September 11th attacks as evidence:

> Revealing though this episode has been of the remarkable strengths of America's "third," or nonprofit, sector, however, it simultaneously revealed the sector's limitations as well. Private voluntary groups, though highly effective in mobilizing individuals to act, are far less equipped to structure the resulting activity. In short order, fragile systems of nonprof-

it response were severely challenged by the enormity of the crisis they confronted in the aftermath of September 11. Individual agencies, concerned about their autonomy, resisted efforts to coordinate their responses, either with each other or with government authorities. Individuals in need of assistance had to navigate a multitude of separate agencies, each with its own eligibility criteria and targeted forms of aid. Inevitably, delays and inequities occurred; many individuals fell through the slats, while others benefited from multiple sources of assistance. What is more, misunderstandings arose between donors, most of whom apparently intended their contributions to be used for immediate relief, and some agencies, most notably the Red Cross, that hoped to squirrel the funds away for longer-term recovery, general institutional support, and other, less visible, disasters down the road. What began as an inspiring demonstration of the power of America's charitable community thus became a demonstration of its shortcomings as well.

In this, the story of the nonprofit sector's response to the crisis of September 11 is emblematic of its position in American life more generally. Long celebrated as a fundamental part of the American heritage, America's nonprofit organizations have suffered from structural shortcomings that limit the role they play. This juxtaposition of strengths and limitations, in turn, has fueled a lively ideological contest over the extent to which we should rely on these institutions to handle critical public needs, with conservatives focusing laser-like on the sector's strengths and liberals often restricting their attention to its weaknesses instead. Through it all, though largely unheralded and perhaps unrecognized by either side, a classically American compromise has taken shape. This compromise was forged early in the nation's history, but it was broadened and solidified in the 1960s. Under it, nonprofit organizations in an ever-widening range of fields were made the beneficiaries of government support to provide a growing array of services—from health care to scientific research—that Americans wanted but were reluctant to have government directly provide. More than any other single factor, this government-nonprofit partnership is responsible for the growth of the nonprofit sector as we know it today. During the last twenty years, however, that compromise has come under considerable assault (2002a, 4-5).

2. . . CONVERSATIONS ON PHILANTHROPY

Salamon's work attempts to show not only how the nonprofit sector can support and improve the modern welfare state, but, more importantly, how the welfare state supports and effectuates the nonprofit sector. Salamon's theory of third-party governance is recognizable as a species of postcommunist scholarship seeking new foundations for strong state action in social and economic planning. Much of today's postcommunist analysis—epitomized by the work of economist Joseph Stiglitz (1994), among others[2]—has turned not toward free and open markets but instead toward the market-based welfare state. Salamon's longstanding advocacy of "third-party government" strikingly resembles this postcommunist justification of the state and likewise relies on an economic critique. Salamon proposes that the rise and evolution of "third-party government" was missed, misinterpreted, or, worse, ignored outright by scholars, largely because of defective economic theory.

Salamon is not the only theorist of the nonprofit sector critical of the standard economic approach. In his intriguing work *The Commons: New Perspectives on Nonprofit Organizations and Voluntary Action*, Roger A. Lohmann (1992, 159-76) agrees that the standard theory fails to understand the nature of the nonprofit organization, but he argues this for reasons that differ substantially from Salamon's.

This paper outlines a critical assessment of the coherence of Salamon's paradigm from a largely Austrian economic perspective (that is, one in the tradition of Ludwig von Mises and F.A. Hayek), examines the potential for Lohmann's suggested revisions, and begins to explore how Austrian economic theory can advance our understanding of the social role of nonprofit voluntary organizations.

We shall proceed by first discussing the motivation behind Salamon's theoretical challenge, one that is rooted in a critique of Burton Weisbrod's economic analysis of nonprofits. We shall then discuss Salamon's attempt to rectify the shortcomings of the Weisbrod model. We shall also explore Lohmann's criticism of the economic theory of nonprofits, which encompasses the attempts by Weisbrod and Salamon. We argue that although some of Lohmann's criticisms are generally correct in spirit, his proposed revisions to mainstream economic analysis (such as his attempt to rectify the classical distinction between "productive" and "unproductive" labor) are unfortunate and can be better developed using the insights of Austrian economic theory. We conclude with a preliminary discussion of the political economy of the nonprofit sector in general.

A Salamonic Paradigm?
Voluntary Failure and Third Party Government

First we must more clearly describe Salamon's approach. Again we will let Salamon's written words speak for him:

> The widespread neglect of the massive growth of government-nonprofit relationships that characterized the 1960s and 1970s was a product not simply of a lack of research but, more fundamentally, of a weakness of theory. Both the theory of the welfare state and the theory of the voluntary sector were deficient, moreover—the former because of its failure to acknowledge the reality of "third-party government" and the latter because of a view of the voluntary sector that emphasized its role as a substitute for the state. Neither perspective left much room for a flourishing government-nonprofit partnership. To come to terms with the reality of widespread government-nonprofit cooperation, therefore, it is necessary to reshape the conceptual lenses through which this reality is perceived, to replace traditional theories of the welfare state with the concept of "third-party government," and to replace prevailing "market failure/government failure" theories of the nonprofit sector with a theory that acknowledges the possibility of "voluntary failure" as well, of inherent limitations of the voluntary sector. Equipped with this alternative set of theoretical lenses, the widespread partnership between government and the nonprofit sector comes into focus not as an aberration, but as a reasonable adaptation to the respective strengths and weaknesses of the voluntary sector and the state. Rather than a phenomenon to be shunned or discouraged, cooperation between government and the voluntary sector emerges from this analysis as a reasonable model to be promoted and improved (1995, 6).

"More than any other single factor," Salamon contends, "this government-nonprofit partnership is responsible for the growth of the nonprofit sector as we know it today" (2002a, 5), and he has developed a wide reputation for a large body of empirical work that appears to support his theory.[3]

Salamon believes his theory provides a new "paradigm"—in the Kuhnian sense (1987, 36; cf. Salamon and Anheier 1996b, 1-7, 119-123)—to explain the evolution of the government-nonprofit partnership, and to justify and promote its continued development. Although the present authors do not share

Salamon's ideological perspective, our purpose here is not to engage in an argument over competing ideological visions.[4] We wish instead to examine Salamon's paradigmatic theory. Salamon attempts to engage in nothing less than a theoretical reconstruction of economic analysis, specifically targeting the notions of market failure and government failure. To this mix he adds his new notion of "voluntary failure." Salamon argues that the (few) economists who have studied the nonprofit sector (most notably, Weisbrod [1977, 1988]) view the complex interconnections between markets, nonprofits, and the state through the wrong theoretical lenses.[5]

The standard literature posits that nonprofit and philanthropic organizations arise in response to both market failures (due to free rider problems) and government failures (due to development of programs that meet the demands of the "majority" of constituents but leave unmet the demands of others).

Burton Weisbrod's thesis (1988, 16-42) is a fairly conventional application of market and government failure analysis to explain the existence—and persistence—of nonprofits in a generally free market system. In short, Weisbrod argues that markets are generally efficient; in specific cases, however, particularly with respect to the production of public goods, the free market alone cannot be expected to generate socially efficient outcomes. Theoretically, at least, government intervention can be used to influence and improve upon (in the sense of generating an optimal or socially efficient result) the provision of public goods by employing its coercive powers to tax free riders (i.e., those who would enjoy consuming a public good but who have little or no incentive to voluntarily pay to obtain it).

Weisbrod suggests that government intervention of this nature tends to work well when consumer demand is homogeneous. In principle, it is a straightforward exercise to determine who gains from the production of a public good (think, for example, of the common, textbook case of national defense), to tax them appropriately, and use those tax revenues to subsidize the production of the public good. On the other hand, when consumer demand is heterogeneous, or diverse, the task is much more complex. Although it might be assumed that most "everybody" in the country enjoys at least a certain level of national defense, not "everybody" enjoys or rides for free on the services provided by Alcoholics Anonymous, the Muscular Dystrophy Association, the Sierra Club, or the Little Sisters of the Poor. While these services *might* display some characteristics of public goods (although we aren't convinced of that), the state cannot effectively, or, rather, efficiently, account for, and accordingly tax and fund, all the confoundedly diverse demands behind these and a panoply of other services. In Weisbrod's view, free riders in the market will prevent—if only unintentionally—the optimal production of these services. This shortcoming typically leads to a call for government intervention to improve upon the outcomes of an otherwise spontaneous market process. But, Weisbrod argues, the government will also fail to place specific taxes on specific people to ensure an optimal allocation—that is, to improve upon the market outcome. Hence, he maintains, nonprofits arise in response to both market and government failure. They emerge as a "substitute" for state intervention in light of efficiency failures in the marketplace.[6]

Salamon (1987, 39; 1992, 125; Salamon and Anheier 1996, 9-10) criticizes Weisbrod for failing to acknowledge an empirically robust partnership between nonprofits and criticizes the state for failing to recognize that nonprofits and the state are not mere substitutes for each other but are in fact symbiotic complements. Salamon suggests that the existing partnership between nonprofits and the state simply cannot be explained or predicted in traditional analytical constructs. Rejecting Weisbrod, Salamon advances the claim that the partnership is fundamentally a response to inefficiencies in the "voluntary," nonprofit sector. "Given a welfare state that is characterized by an extensive pattern of third-party government," he writes, "the persistence of a voluntary sector and widespread government-nonprofit cooperation are not anomalies at all: they are exactly what one would expect" (1987, 43).[7]

At the core of Salamon's self-described paradigm are the notions of efficiency and its converse, inefficiency. By advancing claims that a set of institutions—market, voluntary, or government—are failing, Salamon's approach necessarily employs particular assumptions about the potential efficiency characteristics of those institutions. He needs some benchmark for success. Precisely what does Salamon mean when he speaks of voluntary-sector failure? Just how might nonprofits be inefficient, or how might they be deemed "inherently limited?" What scientific basis does Salamon provide which allows him to conclude that the merging or "partnership" between nonprofits and the welfare state are not only the *consequence* of voluntary sector failure but also an efficient *improvement* within that sector?

To be sure, Salamon recognizes that answers to these kinds of questions are "more conceptual than empirical" (1987, 35). We can't simply go off, willy-nilly, and measure "the" results. We instead require some theoretical framework to give us clues as to *what* (and how) we should be measuring, and how the results are causally related to earlier institutional events and developments. In this sense Salamon's metaphor of needing new theoretical "lenses" is most apt. Nevertheless, we believe (and can argue in detail) that Salamon fails to establish firmly the notion of voluntary-sector failure and the efficiency-enhancing role of the state among nonprofits. Salamon's ideological sentiments favor a robust linkage between nonprofits and the state, but we do not believe he has developed a consistent, positive theory that provides the kind of conceptual framework—a paradigm, in his words—that matches his ideological hope with empirical possibility. We suggest that not only is Salamon's theory defective, but so, too, is the theory that critically influenced Salamon's, that of standard economic analysis, including Weisbrod's.

Weisbrod, Salamon, and most other commentators on the economics of the nonprofit sector draw upon welfare theory, a theoretical model in neoclassical economics that, in our estimation, cannot deliver the goods. This is a strong claim on our behalf, one which requires us to reexamine the standard economic analysis of "market failure."

Success and Failure: A Lesson in Basic Economic Theory

What do economists mean when they say that a market "fails?" And what do they mean when they say that state intervention can alleviate market failure? What, if anything, does government failure mean in this context? Let's briefly examine the theory of market (and government) failure, for Salamon's case for the nonprofit-government partnership cannot be understood without some exposure to the alleged efficiency (and inefficiency) characteristics of markets.

So far we've used the terms "public goods," "market failure," "government failure," and so on rather freely, as if our readers already understand these terms. While this is standard parlance among economists, others often adopt these concepts loosely, and erroneously, for the terms have specific meanings. To better understand these concepts, we must first imagine an idealized economy in which all participants enjoy several limiting assumptions, including the following: full and complete information; zero transaction costs; prices that they take as given (i.e., beyond any individual's or coalition's ability to manipulate). Standard economic analysis has established that individuals within this hypothetical economy will exercise the ability and the incentive to exchange goods and services freely, until *all* mutually beneficial exchanges have been exhausted. Once reached, any further exchange or redistribution of goods, though beneficial to one (or some) parties, will reduce the utility or well-being of other parties.[8] The free market, under these severely limiting assumptions, is considered capable of generating a socially optimal outcome. Although the term "efficiency" has varied meanings, in the theory of standard welfare economics, efficiency is synonymous with Pareto-Optimality—the complete exhaustion of all mutually beneficial exchange possibilities.

In the economics literature, there are formal proofs that under conditions of general competitive equilibrium the economic system will simultaneously achieve production efficiency (i.e., all least-cost technologies will be employed), exchange efficiency (all mutually beneficial gains from exchange will be exhausted), and product-mix efficiency (individuals will receive the bundle of products they are willing to pay for). The Two Fundamental Welfare Theorems follow from these: (1) an economy in general competitive equilibrium is Pareto Efficient, and (2) any Pareto Efficient distribution of resources society desires can be achieved through the market mechanism. When economists speak of "market failure," it is against *this* standard of the first and second welfare theorem that they are judging. Real-world markets, however, might not succeed in fully reaching this optimum.

Market failure, therefore, has a rather refined and specific meaning to economists. Market failure refers to cases where voluntary exchange fails to reach this Pareto-Optimal or "efficient" outcome. The production of a good that creates a negative externality, such as pollution, is a common example.[9] The Weisbrod case for nonprofits focuses, however, on the potential for markets to generate *positive* externalities, and, more specifically, *public goods* problems. *Government failure* comes into play in the context of solving the problems associated with using state action to optimize delivery of public goods. While market failure means a failure of the voluntary exchange process to hit a purely hypothetical optimum, government failure, to be consistent, must mean a failure of the state to compel its citizens to act in ways such that the hypothetical optimum delivery of public goods is realized.

Weisbrod's work has the virtue of using the market failure concept correctly. It seems to us that he also uses the concept of government failure generally correctly. Relying on these concepts, Weisbrod views the nonprofit sector as a remedy for both market and government failure, especially in the delivery of highly diversified or heterogeneous public goods:

> Dealing with diversity—which is fundamentally a problem of information—is a major problem for government. If all consumers had identical demands for public action—whether for trust-type, consumer-protection services, or for other collective goods—this problem would disappear. When demand is diverse, though, whatever quantities and qualities of services government provides will oversatisfy some people and undersatisfy others. Can the nonprofit form of institution respond? (1988, 25).

Our problem with this approach, and that of welfare theory in general, is the misplaced concreteness that too readily allows the confusion of economic models with reality. Even if problems of calculation and taxation could be solved in instances of homogeneous demand for certain goods (and we treat this hypothesis with enormous skepticism), there is simply no way that citizens, economists, policymakers, or anyone else can possibly know people's unexpressed "demands" in real, existing economies, *regardless* of whether we have *a priori* beliefs that those demands might be homogeneous for some goods and heterogeneous for others.[10]

How Does Any of This Relate to the Viability of the Nonprofit Sector?

If you have followed our outline thus far, you are probably asking that very question. The critical claim that Weisbrod makes is that nonprofits can mitigate government failure. Alas, however, he doesn't demonstrate that nonprofits generate the optimal outcome in light of government failure, nor that nonprofits come "closer" to the optimal outcome. In fact, he *cannot* demonstrate that real-world nonprofits do either of these things. Neither he, nor any other economist, knows what the Pareto Optimal point is for *any* aspect of society. Hence, our approach to understanding the existence and action of nonprofit organizations seriously questions the value, and purpose, of the Pareto-Optimality benchmark that undergirds the market failure/government failure analysis. This is not an argument against nonprofits. Indeed, if we are to arrive at a more vigorous and theoretically viable understanding of non-profit action, we must confront head-on the supposition that nonprofits emerge merely to make up for failures of the market and the state.

Salamon's Notion of Voluntary Failure

Salamon's new paradigm is critical of the market failure/government fail-ure explanation of nonprofits, too, but for reasons fundamentally different from ours. He seeks not to radically question standard welfare theory, but to revise it to account for yet a *third* form of failure—that of the voluntary sec-tor itself. Standard economists chatter a great deal about failure in the market and state sectors, but Salamon adds that if the voluntary or "third" sector is a significant parallel institutional sector, perhaps it, too, is prone to failure.

The project of proposing voluntary failure would seem to require, then, a careful adaptation of the standard welfare theory of "failure" in the con-text of the voluntary sector. Nevertheless, we haven't come across any men-tion of Pareto Optimality in Salamon's writing, negative or positive.[11] His case for voluntary failure, it appears, depends on the implications of data rather than theory. Salamon's reading of Weisbrod suggests, to him, that the standard theory cannot account for the empirical interconnections between the welfare state and nonprofit organizations—that is, for the fact that non-profits are often involved in the direct delivery of services, supported through compulsory state actions through subsidies and other measures. Salamon claims that this "partnership" remains a factual anomaly in the Weisbrod model. "Not only does this partnership have deep historical roots," Salamon maintains, "it also has a strong theoretical rationale" (1989, 204). He goes so far as to say that this "partnership" was a "central organ-izing principle of the American welfare state" (1989, 205),[12] and he believes that these observations establish a sufficient theoretical explanation.

Salamon's case rests upon his concept of "voluntary failure" and, because he juxtaposes this concept against market and government failure, an implicit acceptance of Pareto Optimality. But he apparently misunder-stands the objective of the government economic policy solution to the pos-itive externality and public goods problem. He claims that:

The central problem with the theory of the welfare state as it has been applied to the American context is its failure to differentiate between government's role as a provider of funds and direction, and government's role as a deliverer of services...

Far from the bureaucratic monolith pictured in conventional theories, the welfare state in the American context makes use of a wide variety of third parties to carry out governmental functions. The result is an elaborate system of "third-party government"... in which government shares a substantial degree of its discretion over the spending of public funds and the exercise of public authority with third-party implementers (1987, 41).

Salamon calls for a distinction between the case for government *taxation and funding* of goods associated with positive externalities and public-good characteristics and government *production* of those goods. Nevertheless, he fails sufficiently to distinguish funding from production. He observes a world where funding and production/delivery are often separate and labels that phenomenon "third-party government." He then claims that standard welfare economics cannot conceptually explain this assignment of government function to external nonprofit institutions—hence the empirical "anomaly" he sets out to explain in his own theory. Unfortunately, Salamon shares a common but erroneous belief that the standard economist's case necessarily involves a combination of government funding and production.

James Buchanan, in one of the landmark works on the subject, stated clearly that funding and production of public goods can be legitimately separate functions:

Collectivization, or public organization, refers to the provision of the good, its financing and distribution among separate demanders. Nothing in the discussion implies anything at all about the actual *organization of production.* Whether or not the good is purchased from privately organized firms and individuals in the domestic economy, purchased from privately or publicly organized supplying agencies abroad, or produced directly by government itself should depend on an efficiency calculus which compares these various alternatives. Collectivization of the supply, to meet individuals' private demands, says nothing about the relative efficiency of producing the good in any one of the several ways. This is a self-evident point, and it would not be necessary to mention here were it not for the widespread confusion that seems to exist (1968, 186).[13]

Salamon's hope to explain "third-party government" with a new paradigm—one that can finally begin to account for this "anomaly" of government
funding and third-party production/delivery of public goods (in other places, he
calls it an aberration [1995, 6])—is without theoretical support. Simply stated,
there is no anomaly at all, for nothing in standard economic analysis suggests,
as a general principle, that government intervention used to correct for market
failures necessitates government *production* of those "failed" goods and services. Instead, standard analysis typically suggests that the government can
improve the efficiency of the market by forcing free riders to pay, through
taxes, for the goods that they enjoy. The specific organization of production—
a matter of determining property-rights arrangements as to who will produce
and supply the good or service in question—is an altogether separate matter,
one that, in the standard analysis, rests with the relative costs and technical
efficiencies of the private sector as compared to the public sector. Salamon's
interpretation of nonprofit production of public goods as an extension of legitimate functions of government is an unfortunate misunderstanding of basic
economic theory, and it leads him to misinterpret the implications of the data.

Now, that in itself doesn't require us to reject entirely Salamon's concept
of "voluntary failure." The standard "paradigm," as it were, has already
accounted for and explained nongovernment production of public and other
goods with significant positive externalities. Its theoretical "lenses," as it
were, have already observed what Salamon otherwise considers unobserv-
able. Perhaps, however, Salamon's "voluntary failure" concept can be fitted
into the standard analysis, and thereby clarify and shore up the normative
defense of government-nonprofit collaboration that he has tried to develop
over the years.

Salamon advances claims that the voluntary sector is "inherently" limited, that it will likely offer services that "will be less than those society considers optimal," and that it "has serious drawbacks as a generator of a reliable stream of resources to respond adequately to community needs." He at
least implicitly accepts the Paretian benchmark when he acknowledges the
possibility of both market and government failure. To be consistent, then, he
must accept that same benchmark to speak meaningfully of a "voluntary failure" to generate an "adequate" and "optimal" level of nonprofit services.
Otherwise, what else do these terms mean? To suggest that government-nonprofit collaboration improves upon the voluntary sector's outcomes, that it

overcomes its inherent limitations, requires some kind of benchmark of success that is consistent with the other two failure concepts. But Salamon develops nothing of the kind, in his 1987 paper or after. He instead depends upon a tremendous amount of empirical work to justify his theoretical conclusion that third-party government is a reasonable arrangement in light of market, government, and voluntary failure.

Here we would reiterate our observation that the entire welfare economics framework is flawed with unrealistic assumptions as well as with unrealizable goals and expectations for policymakers and government bureaucrats. Adding the voluntary-sector failure concept does not noticeably improve the theory. Some of the criticisms made by Roger Lohmann seem to be on point here, and we shall turn to his account shortly. In our view, the Pareto framework in general, and the effort of Weisbrod to apply it to nonprofits in particular, is an example of misplaced concreteness. Weisbrod's effort and those of mainstream economists in this regard have at least the "virtue" of clearly articulating at the purely conceptual, theoretical level what optimality and failure mean. Salamon's effort only muddies the waters.

Salamon accepts in principle the notions of market failure and social optimality and advances claims that "third-party government" can propel the for-profit and nonprofit sectors toward a socially optimal outcome. However, he has not clearly articulated what he means by the concepts of optimality and failure. If he has the Pareto-Optimal criteria in mind, then he hasn't made any effort to demonstrate that the modern welfare state's funding of nonprofit services has propelled our system closer toward the socially optimal outcome. None of his empirical work has demonstrated, nor can it demonstrate, that a government-nonprofit partnership is closer to, farther from, or at a social optimum; nor has his work demonstrated that the disentangling of the wonderful panoply of nonprofits away from the state (a more recent development he laments) has pulled the system farther away from the socially optimal result. Salamon's addition to welfare theory—the concept of voluntary failure—has not demonstrated that the nonprofit sector fails to reach Pareto Optimality. Nor, toward an equally important goal, has this concept explained how the partnership between the nonprofit sector and the state can, even in pure theory, bring us closer to the Pareto Optimum. He makes these kinds of claims without introducing a methodology to provide either clear theoretical or empirical measures of the social optimum.

Perhaps Salamon has not offered a theoretical demonstration because he doesn't accept the Pareto-Optimal criteria. He may have a completely different understanding of what a socially optimal outcome means—but that does not square with his acceptance of the standard "market failure" concept. In addition, it clearly raises the obvious question of why hasn't he bothered to articulate—if only at the conceptual level—what he means when developing his own optimality criteria.

Salamon is indeed correct in asserting that the "real answer" to the questions that he seeks to address in his body of research is "more conceptual than empirical," but the bulk of his work since formulating his theory has been predominantly empirical, guided by his concept of voluntary failure. If his conceptual framework is, as we argue, flawed, then his selection and interpretation of the empirical data are also in question. On this point we find additional support in Smith (2000).

Toward an Alternative Theory: Lohmann on the Commons

We have thus far questioned both the knowledge assumptions and the theoretical coherence of the "failure project." Roger A. Lohmann (1992, 159-160) also questions the failure theories of Salamon and Weisbrod, and the economic theory of the nonprofit sector in general, on the basis of the model's assumptions. His criticism differs from what we have provided so far, and his proposed alternative reformulation of the theory is worth exploring.

While our criticism focuses on assumptions regarding the knowledge available to both citizens and to the economic theorists developing real-world "solutions" to less than Pareto-Optimal outcomes, Lohmann criticizes the failure project for apparently grafting a theory of narrow self-interest and profit-seeking onto a social domain that substantially differs from commercial market activity. This domain still claims no universally accepted defining terminology: although "nonprofit sector" is a common usage, Richard Cournelle (1965) first proposed that it might be called the "independent sector," Salamon calls it the "voluntary sector," and Lohmann himself refers to it as "the commons."[14] Lohmann's effort to rename and create a distinct theoretical space for the sector is important: while assumptions that individuals pursue narrow self-interests might be suitable for the study of competitive commercial activity (the for-profit sector), Lohmann stresses—correctly in our view—that human action in general is not exclusively of the narrow, self-interested variety stereotypically ascribed to *homo economicus*. "The calculus of costs and benefits," Lohmann laments, "has become a universal index to what is rational" (1992, 15). Lohmann asserts that rationality is much richer: "The pursuit of common goods is rational behavior, albeit distinguishable from the self-interested pursuit of profit that characterizes markets" (1992, 272-73). Reducing rationality to an overly restricted view of rational choice and calculative utility or profit maximization leads, at best, to an economic theory that treats nonprofits "as if" they were for-profit firms (1992, 16, 38), which, of course, "in the process dissolve[s] the very thing that is to be explained" (1992, 129). This logic is remarkably similar to the critiques of standard economic theory of perfect competition made by F. A. Hayek and Ronald Coase: if we assume for-profit firms act "as if" they faced perfect and complete information and zero transaction costs, we dissolve any reason for for-profit firms to exist at all. Lohmann likewise observes that the standard approach of economists leads to contradictions in market theory and also systematically underrates the potential efficiency of nonprofits compared to the ideal efficiency characteristics of competitive, for-profit firms:

> This particular construction of the theory of nonprofit organizations begins with the critical assumption that nonprofits are a flawed or incomplete form of for-profit organization. Advocates of this position tend to assume, based on the absence of a consistent performance measure, that nonprofit organizations as a class are inherently more inefficient in the conduct of their affairs than comparable for-profit organizations (1992, 26).

Lohmann proposes that a theory of nonprofits ought to understand more clearly the interactive nature of individuals organized in nonprofit associations rather than "treat them as rather odd, intangible, and inefficient forms of productive enterprise" (1992, 164), for those are evaluative categories that are not so much the conclusions of careful research as they are biases already embedded into the theory's starting assumptions. *Homo economicus* would rarely find value in establishing or joining nonprofits unless, perhaps, he had something up his sleeve![15]

We appreciate and agree with Lohmann's call for movement beyond the narrow neoclassical modeling of nonprofits. He believes that "some of the independent research efforts and work in nontraditional disciplines may have major implications for the rethinking of nonprofit studies" (1992, 8), and that "it is unlikely that these conceptual problems can be resolved within economics alone" (1992, 39). Lohmann's work is refreshingly eclectic, and draws from the theories of meaningful action found in Max Weber and Alfred Schutz (1992, 47-48), the hermeneutics of Hans-Georg Gadamer and Richard Bernstein (1992, 262), and Kenneth Boulding's call for an economic analysis that can account for the motives of love and fear, as opposed to a purely utility-maximizing calculus (1992, 170). As two (outlier) economists who have been inspired by the work of all of these individuals and have tried to draw their work into Austrian economic theory, we must admit we have a modest bias toward Lohmann's efforts.[16] That said, we find that Lohmann unfortunately wishes to resurrect some other fundamentally flawed assumptions of classical economic theory. In other words, he falls short not by pointing toward non-economic social theories, but instead by a peculiar return to classical economic theory. Once again we will see that a critical stumbling block for nonprofit theory exists in our understanding of the organization of production by nonprofit firms.

Is Unproductive Labor Common in the Commons?

Lohmann puts it the following way:
An adequate economic model for analysis of the commons ought to begin by studying actual economic institutions, like donations and endowments, and by adjusting or suspending three conventional economic assumptions: scarcity, production, and maximization. The economics of common goods does not require rejecting the concept of scarcity entirely. However, acknowledgment of the moral and rational consequences of affluence or social surplus is important (1992, 160-61).

Lohmann supports what he calls "existential" scarcity—basically, the universal fact that people must choose, as wants exceed what is available (1992, 161). So far, so good. That's what all economists mean (or should mean) by the term. He questions the role of models wedded exclusively to maximization (1992, 163), and suggests the concept should lose its "privileged position" as a universal approach to social action. We generally agree with him here, too.[17] He slips a bit—as many non-economists do—with his use of the term *surplus*, but our concern is chiefly with his use of the term *production*.

Hearkening back to Adam Smith's *Wealth of Nations*, Lohmann writes,
Nonprofit economics grounded in failure theory treats nonprofit organizations by analogy with (as if they were) the profit-oriented firms of micro-
economics... Adam Smith's distinction between productive and unproductive labor...is ignored or overturned in the contemporary concept of volunteer labor [cites Weisbrod]. Such an approach is defensible in the analysis
of revenue-generating nonprofit firms like hospitals; nursing homes; and
some museums, theaters and concert halls, where clear-cut prices are
exchanged for recognizable products. However, the rationale for treating
"unproductive" (non-revenue) membership clubs; donative charities; and
a broad range of other religious, scientific, or artistic commons as if they
were commercial firms is highly questionable. Yet because of the widespread commitment of nonprofit economics to the market firm analogy, no
other economic models of the commons have received serious consideration. *A major project confronting nonprofit and voluntary action
researchers, therefore, is to begin the construction of a genuine economics
of common goods premised on more plausible and relevant assumptions*
(1992, 160; our emphasis).

We agree especially with Lohmann's last point. The instrumental nature
of mainstream economic theory is not concerned with the descriptive realism
of its assumptions, but focuses economists on their ability to make accurate
predictions. Lohmann's argument suggests that instrumentalism has largely
run its course—at least with regard to nonprofits—and, moreover, proceeds
with biases that cast doubt on the viability and value of nonprofits before the
research is undertaken.

Despite our agreement with the central thrust of this critique, we are
troubled by Lohmann's appeal to Adam Smith. Is Smith's distinction between
productive and unproductive labor something that a new economic approach
to nonprofits ought to reconsider? It, and Smith's corresponding definition of
wealth, have been sources of discussion in the nonprofit literature, including
the work of Severyn Bruyn (1991, 322-325), who laments that Smith denigrat-
ed the service sector and created a strictly material notion of wealth that he
believes haunts us to this day.[18]

Smith, and the early classicals in general, confined "wealth" to material
goods production.[19] Smith differentiated material goods from services, and
argued, if only as an analytical convenience, that labor used to produce mate-

rial goods was categorically different from labor employed for services. For Smith, labor is *productive* if it increases the output of material goods (wealth); it is *unproductive* if it only provides services.[20] Productive labor is that which creates vendible commodities.

Lohmann supports Smith's distinction because he believes that the mainstream economics literature "equates all types of human behavior with production," which he believes "must be explicitly rejected in the case of the commons" (1992, 162). Regrettably, in our opinion, he embraces Smith's distinction and argues that because nonprofits are not producing vendible commodities (recall, nonprofits, as we are using the term, don't produce anything for sale on the market), the labor involved in nonprofit associations (the commons) is "unproductive" and therefore not amenable to standard profit-maximization analysis. In other words, it's a fundamentally different category of labor that can't be pigeonholed into the standard maximization model. It is, using Smith's term, *unproductive* labor. For Lohmann, the neoclassical treatment continues to ignore this crucial distinction, which may prove to be a good point at which to begin developing a more coherent theory of production of nonprofit "goods."

The Austrian Contribution

In our view, returning to Smith's distinction between productive and unproductive labor won't help us differentiate the purpose of for-profit firms from nonprofit activity. There is of course a peculiar irony, if we follow Lohmann, that the promotion of the nonprofit sector would imply the exalting of "unproductive" labor, when, in fact, such services can be remarkably productive. But more importantly, we believe that the distinction between "productive" and "unproductive" labor makes absolutely no sense. This is precisely where an Austrian understanding of wealth, production, and ultimately calculation can contribute to the development of an alternative theory of nonprofits such as Lohmann, Salamon, and others seek.

What is wealth?

In its broadest sense, wealth is simply *anything* that a person values. Smith and the classicals developed an economic theory to try to explain material wealth, which led them to make the distinction between labor that produces material things—vendible commodities—and labor that produces services. By contrast, the subjective theory of value articulated by Austrian economists holds that wealth is whatever a person strives for: it consists not only of material things (from food, water, and shelter to fast cars, video games, and money), but also of nonmaterial goods (such as love, respect, intelligence, historic preservation, beauty, and so forth). As we have stated elsewhere (Heyne, Boettke, and Prychitko 2003, 18), equating wealth strictly with material things makes no sense in a theory of choice, and must be rejected at its root.

What is production?

In simplest terms, production is the creation of wealth, the creation of anything we value. Of course, we typically picture the construction of new buildings, roads, bridges, and the like as productive activities. New things— new human artifacts—have been created. But production is not to be limited to the production of new things. Simple acts of trading already-produced items (as in barter, for example) are productive because they increase the wealth of both trading parties. Each individual in a voluntary trade sacrifices something they value for something they value more highly. Each individual gains (or, at least expects to gain) more by engaging in the exchange; otherwise, it would not be voluntarily undertaken. Most modern economists have this understanding of wealth and production in mind, even if they tend to focus largely on the production of material wealth (see Heyne, Boettke, and Prychitko 2003, 17-20).

Why doesn't the productive/unproductive labor distinction make sense?

The restriction of wealth to material things as a result of the differentiation of productive and unproductive labor is simply too limiting. Ludwig von Mises stated this clearly in his 1933 work, *Epistemological Problems in Economics:*

Because the classical economists were able to explain only the action of businessmen and were helpless in the face of everything that went beyond it, their thinking was oriented toward bookkeeping, the supreme expression of the rationality of the businessman (but not that of the consumer). Whatever cannot be entered into the businessman's accounts they were unable to accommodate in their theory. This explains several of their ideas—for example, their position in regard to personal services. The performance of a service which caused no increase in value that could be explained in the ledger of the businessman had to appear to them as unproductive. Only thus can it be explained why they regarded the attainment of the greatest monetary profit possible as the goal of economic action. Because of the difficulties occasioned by the paradox of value, they were unable to find a bridge from the realization, which they owed to utilitarianism, that the goal of action is an increase of pleasure and a decrease of pain, to the theory of value and price. Therefore, they were unable to comprehend any change in well-being that cannot be valued in money in the account books of the businessman (1981, 175).

[W]ith the scheme of the *homo economicus* classical economics comprehended only one side of man—the economic, materialistic side. It observed him only as a man engaged in business, not as a consumer of economic goods (1981, 180).

Mises argued that economics, as a theory of choice, cannot restrict itself to the calculative rationality personified by businesspeople—call it simply *homo economicus*—and claim universal applicability. Mises called for a *praxeology* (1981, 180), a general theory of choice that does not succumb to distinguishing choice in a heterogeneous way, and later attempted a full-blown praxeological theory (1966).

What is Calculation?

One of Mises's greatest achievements was in developing a theory of economic calculation. In the Austrian tradition, calculation has a highly refined meaning. It is not merely measurement, as in some input-output flow chart. After all, Soviet planners could measure how much land, labor, fertilizer, tractors, and so on it took to produce a ton of wheat on the collective farms. But they couldn't calculate the added value of that effort to determine whether they had used those resources efficiently and productively. Lacking market-generated prices, they had no way of solving, with Mises, "the task of allocating [scarce resources] to those employments in which they can render the best service" (1966, 207). They couldn't determine whether or not their production plans were worth the cost—whether they generated a positive net improvement in wealth. This makes for an economic and social disaster, for the efforts of planners *can't* coincide with the interests of the socialist system's citizens. They lack the knowledge to plan the economy successfully because they lack the ability to calculate.

Measurable data—call it simply information—does not in itself allow for rational economic calculation, as Mises employs the term. In fact, he goes so far as to say, "the distinctive mark of economic calculation is that it is neither based upon nor related to anything which could be characterized as measurement" (1966, 209). This sounds strange, but Mises argues that measurement implies a fixed unit of measure (say, the length of a yardstick), but calculation requires market-generated prices, and prices themselves are not immutable units; they change over time, whereas a yardstick doesn't.

This language can be confusing to non-economists, so we shall forgo any lengthy discussion and jump to the bottom line: economic calculation, as Mises and Austrian economists in general use the term, is only possible with monetary prices established in markets. Calculation of profit (or loss)—the residual or added monetary value of a firm's activity—can be determined only by market prices. Mises insists that "money prices are the only vehicle of economic calculation" (1966, 201; also see 208-209, 229).

Exactly what is calculated?

Mises further insists that "Monetary calculation is not the calculation, and certainly not the measurement, of value" (1981, 160). Monetary calculation allows decision makers—say, for-profit entrepreneurs—to calculate the expected monetary *residual* of their efforts, the total revenues from the total costs of their efforts. It also allows them to assess after the fact whether their expectations were realized (in the form of a monetary profit or loss). Monetary calculation does not generate an objective measure of value—for value, in an economic theory of choice, resides in the eyes of the choosers (though, admittedly, it can have an intersubjective dimension).

Can not-for-profit organizations calculate?

Hence, the dependence of calculation upon market-generated prices does not necessarily handicap not-for-profit firms. Recall our distinction between nonprofit organizations and not-for-profit firms. Not-for-profit firms face market prices for their inputs, and charge a market price for their service or product. As long as their inputs and outputs are priced through the voluntary exchange of providers and recipients (a "market mechanism," as it were), the expected residual (or profit, distribution issues aside) can be calculated, as well as the realized residual (the actual profit or loss).

For these kinds of not-for-profit organizations—ones that price their services—calculation can and does occur. Perhaps this is why Lohmann places them outside the realm he calls the commons. The donors can receive, in principle, a calculative measure of the (monetary) value added that occurs, or fails to occur, in specific not-for-profit organizations, and therefore have a guide for framing their grant-making choices.[21]

Most noncommercial voluntary organizations, however, do not calculate.
And *here's* what Lohmann is really trying to point out. Voluntary nonprofit organizations and associations may, and surely do, purchase or lease inputs on the market, and are therefore guided by prices at that stage, but they don't price their "product" or service (however they define it). They engage in unilateral transfers, providing a scarce service to others without the exchange of money (or any other commodity, for that matter) in return (Boulding 1981, ch. 1). They do have access to market processes (and, of course, political processes). Being "in" the commons does not imply they are divorced from other social institutions and processes. Yet, although nonprofits can undertake *measurements*, and, if encouraged, a rational assessment of their outcomes (using both quantitative and qualitative means), they have no way of calculating the realized results against the expected results. Nonprofit organizations and associations cannot, in other words, calculate the residual or monetary value-added of their endeavor, *ex ante* or *ex post*. In this sense, *nonprofit* is a better term for those that don't price their service or product. There is *no* calculated monetary profit.

We suggest that the distinction between calculative and noncalculative action is more productive, as it were, than Smith's distinction between productive and unproductive labor. But there remains a troublesome aspect of these kinds of nonprofits in the very fact that calculation does not and cannot exist. The absence of such calculation implies that entrepreneurs who create and executives who manage nonprofit firms may indeed be handicapped in their ability to demonstrate the efficiency or inefficiency of their activities. If we stick with Mises's definition and understanding of calculation—which we want to do—there is either calculation or there isn't. There are no "proxies for calculation": issues of trust, reputation, satisfaction, and so on might serve as effective guides to action, but they cannot serve as sources for calculation itself. Market prices are a necessary and sufficient institution that allows for calculation (although inflation can severely distort that role). Pseudo-calculation means, in effect, no calculation, in the Austrian perspective. Without a priced service, the agents of nonprofit organizations and their donors might engage in pseudo-calculation, but let's understand that really means no calculation. We suggest it would be vain for theorists or practitioners to try to discover or invent some kind of pseudo-calculative proxy for price and thereby claim that they have "solved the calculation problem" in the nonprofit sector. This also implies that the search for a calculation of "social wealth," "social return on investment," or even a standard measurement, is problematic.[22]

Does this problem imply that the largest set of nonprofit firms are prone to coordination failure?

Salamon, of course, has his own answer to this question, related to his use of the voluntary failure concept. As we have declared above, however, we believe that applying notions of failure, which are by definition linked to concepts of economic efficiency, creates a problematic and misleading approach to a theory of nonprofit activity.

We recognize that at first blush our suggestion that individuals in nonprofit organizations are engaged more in a noncalculative activity might be troublesome for economists who consider calculation to be a necessary condition for rational and effective human activity. In a sense, when studying the nonprofit sector we are moving from the domain of economics (and calculation) to the broader realm of praxeology, the general theory of human action, as Mises himself distinguished these terms (1966, 234). This avoidance of reductionism is what Lohmann really has in mind, and justifiably so. Mises argues that economics is the subset of praxeology that deals with calculative action (1966, 199), but he affirms that not all human action is "economic" and calculative (1966, 231). When we consider the nonprofit sector, we are moving in part into that realm of human action that straightforward economic theory, with its emphasis on calculation, can't quite capture. Economics is, Mises insists, the most elaborated subset of a more general theory of human action (1966, 3). But economic calculation is not *synonymous* with rational human action. It is one terribly important *kind* of rational action that evolves with commercial society, but it would be a great mistake to claim that only calculative action engenders rational, coordinating properties.

The following statements by Mises (1966, 214-15), which we shall quote at length, should help clarify what's at stake in our exploration of the non-profit sector (we interject in brackets where we deem it helpful):

Economic calculation cannot comprehend things, which [like the services of nonprofits] are not sold and bought against money.

There are things which are not for sale and for whose acquisition sacrifices other than money and money's worth must be expended. He who wants to train himself for great achievements must employ many means, some of which may require expenditure of money. But the essential things to be devoted to such an endeavor are not purchasable. Honor, virtue, glory, and likewise vigor, health, and life itself play a role in action both as means and as ends, but they do not enter into economic calculation.

There are things which cannot at all be evaluated in money, there are other things which can be appraised in money only with regard to a fraction of the value assigned to them. The appraisal of an old building must disregard its artistic and historical eminence *so far* as [our emphasis] these qualities are not a source of proceeds in money goods vendible. What touches a man's heart only and does not induce other people to make sacrifices for its attainment remains outside the pale of economic calculation.

However, all this does not in the least impair the usefulness of economic calculation. Those things which do not enter into the items of accountancy and calculation are either ends or goods of the first order. No calculation is required to acknowledge them fully and make due allowance to them. All that acting man needs in order to make his choice is to contrast them with the total amount of costs their acquisition or preservation requires. [And here Mises turns to a rather remarkable example.] Let us assume that a town council has to decide between two water supply projects. One of them implies the demolition of a historical landmark, while the other at the cost of an increase in money expenditure spares this landmark. The fact that the feelings which recommend the conservation of the monument cannot be estimated in a sum of money does not in any way impede the councilmen's decision. The values that are not reflected in any monetary exchange ratio are, on the contrary, by this very fact lifted into a particular position which makes the decision rather easier [yes, *easier!*]. No complaint is less justified than the lamentation that the computation methods of the market do not comprehend things not vendible. Moral and aesthetic values do not suffer any damage on account of this fact.

Mises's acknowledgement that calculation is not required to make a rational decision to spare the town landmark hits the heart of the issue. Nonprofits are not isolated islands of human activity within the voluntary sector—the commons. Like another institution, the family, participants in nonprofits are themselves embedded in the institutional matrix of the market economy. Nonprofits have prices to guide them, particularly when purchasing or leasing inputs. In this way they can coordinate their resource demands with the supplies of resource providers, and they can and do participate in the knowledge-disseminating features of the market process. Although they cannot calculate the value added of their efforts, they can determine whether their specific goals and efforts are worthwhile. Nonprofits have to persuade prospective donors that their effort is worthwhile, of course. Rather than persuade them with the lure or calculated signal of monetary profit, however, they must turn to noncalculative but measurable or assessable means. The lack of economic calculation does not in itself create any impediment to coordination. Likewise, there can be no theoretically sustainable notion of "voluntary failure" such as that proposed by Salamon. The objection might be made, however, that application of a subjective theory of value as proposed here cannot help produce overall efficient allocation of philanthropic resources (or of tax-generated resources for welfare). Here, more broad accomplishment of plan fulfillment must suffice in the necessary absence of some more comprehensive yet undefinable and unattainable standard of social optimality. Even against the Pareto standard, there is little justification for criticizing nonprofit firms as failing in terms of efficiency.

We suggest that the managers of nonprofits, "social entrepreneurs," and their donors are able to make rational decisions about the effectiveness of their activities even though they cannot calculate the value added in a monetary sense—calculation being, again, a dollar measure of the total costs of their efforts and the total benefits of their efforts, the difference being monetary profit (or loss).[23] We would add that they would have a greater incentive than government officials to assess effectiveness, because unlike Mises's councilmen they cannot rely upon the power to tax. Instead, they must depend upon the voluntary contributions of their donors. This, of course, is problematic in our society, where many nonprofits often bypass the responsibility of persuasion and voluntary exchange and instead seek support from the state (not unlike many private business enterprises). In this regard, to accept Salamon's advocacy of third-party government, which in effect seeks to legitimate nonprofit firms as arms of state action, would further weaken the effectiveness of nonprofit organizations by encouraging them to engage more in political rent-seeking than in marketplace persuasion.

The Bigger Picture: Governance and the Nonprofit Sector

With Lohmann, we believe that the nonprofit sector is viable and, we should add, productive. But we think Lohmann's appeal to the distinction between productive and unproductive labor as a central theoretical premise should be jettisoned in favor of the Austrian distinction between calculative and noncalculative rationality. This leads us back to the normative issue of whether the commons should be a largely independent sector, or whether its "partnership" with the state is a promising development.

Independence and Constitutional Constraint

A promising theoretical alternative to Salamon's "third party government," we suggest, would build on the distinction between the financing and provision of so-called public goods that Salamon considers so anomalous in standard economics. As we argued above, this distinction is not anomalous in the least, and the distinction is, in fact, crucial to keep in mind. James Buchanan (1975) has distinguished in his work between the protective state (national defense, courts, and police), the productive state (provision of public goods such as roads and bridges), and the redistributive state (interest group politics, rent-seeking, and welfare policies). In the Buchanan constitutional political economy project, the task is to simultaneously empower the protective and productive state while constraining the redistributive state through constitutional construction. The problem, of course, is whether such a balancing act can indeed ever be accomplished once the power to tax is established. Unless there are strong constraints on the expansion of state power, the natural proclivity of the state would be to use its taxation power to benefit some at the expense of others.

Kenneth Boulding (1969, 482) recognized that "the private grants economy may be justified primarily in terms of it being a check or countervailing power to the public grants economy." Salamon fails to appreciate Buchanan's concerns and Boulding's insight—in part, we believe, because his new "paradigm" doesn't take sufficient account of the unintended consequences of human action.

In a genuinely free society, the voluntary sector should play a critical role in reinforcing the constitutional constraints that limit government to those activities, and only those activities, to which it has a reasonable claim to engage and use its coercive power of taxation and monopoly provision. Granted, this is not the intended purpose or goal of nonprofit and philanthropic enterprise. Voluntary-sector associations are organized to serve particular human needs. Rarely, if ever, do the agents of such associations have in mind the objective of limiting the compulsory powers of the state. But that's precisely what makes this function so elusive. A robust, interconnected system of nonprofits and other civil-society associations can—as an unintended consequence—function to reinforce constitutional constraints on the state simply by providing goods and services without state involvement or intervention. And it is this unplanned, though fertile, feature of the voluntary sector in a free society that is ignored by standard analysis, and by Salamon's approach, despite the fact that it was observed by Alexis de Tocqueville prior to the growth of the modern welfare state.

Many people misunderstand the argument made by economists such as Buchanan, Friedman, and Hayek concerning the role of government. Such "libertarian" economists are typically less concerned with the scale of government than the scope of government. Of course, the absolute size of government can be a concern, given fiscal realities, but the primary concern of these economists is the activities government attempts to tackle. There are activities in which government should not be involved in a free society. In the United States, for example, the general population would object strongly if government attempted to take over the financing and production of religion and perhaps of news services, but the majority have not objected to government financing and provision of educational services (a consent now being reexamined by a burgeoning school choice movement). It is not our purpose here to debate these issues, but simply to argue that Salamon's lack of conceptual clarity leads him to err in explaining the functional significance of the voluntary sector in a society of free and responsible individuals.

The voluntary sector, moreover, ceases to serve this function—and loses the capacity to do so—when organizations within it partner with the coercive powers of the state. At that point, neither government nor market shortcomings can be overcome by this "third sector" because, instead, nonprofit organizations are transformed into rent-seeking entities dependent on tax finance rather than the voluntary contributions of individual donors. As client-partners of the state, many contemporary not-for-profit and nonprofit organizations provide goods and services, but no longer sustain the necessary feedback and disciplinary mechanisms to ensure that good intentions are channeled in directions that generate desired results. In the absence of both calculation and other measures of program effectiveness, modern nonprofits rely increasingly on political effectiveness, which inherently weakens their independent character. This shortchanges society of the valuable information and learning that should arise from independent nonprofit institutions.

Institutions and information

Hayek's work encourages readers to consider the capacity of people to learn within alternative institutional settings. Essential to the learning process is blunt and continual feedback to actors so they may become informed about the effectiveness of previous actions. In social interactions, of course, human intentions do not automatically equal the realized results; thus, in economic analysis, a results orientation must trump considerations of intent and moral intuition. Actors must be disciplined to align their behavior with desired outcomes, and they must be continually informed about how best to do so. In a for-profit setting, actors receive signals through the price system, helping them align their incentives and actions appropriately. In the political setting of democratic politics, political actors are disciplined—in theory, at least—through the vote mechanism. In an independent nonprofit sector, actors must rely on the signal of voluntary contributions and construct measures of output to show that desired results are, in fact, being achieved. This is an admittedly difficult project, not only for the real-world participants within this sector but also for theorists striving to explain the coordinating properties of the sector.[24]

Like the nonprofit sector, politics does not work as smoothly as theory might predict. The vote mechanism is not as effective at disciplining politicians as we might like, because of various public-choice problems. Markets, while undoubtedly very effective at disciplining actors, cannot be relied upon to price many products that are nevertheless essential to creating a vibrant and just community. Thus, it is important to delineate the appropriate role of government and look at the functional significance of nonprofits in filling the gap left by government and the market. But again, the voluntary sector can only serve this role if it abstains from or is denied the use of tax-derived resources.

Cooperation and Competition

Hayek (1979), building on the work of Cornuelle (1965), argues that an independent nonprofit sector has great potential for ensuring social cooperation by mobilizing individuals to work to improve the community environment; health, education, and work opportunities; and even the basic codes of conduct we rely on in our daily intercourse. Ironically, Cornuelle contends that as the voluntary sector gained the power to accomplish more things thanks to technological innovations in the 20th century, ideological shifts led to a situation where more of these activities were turned over to the government rather than the voluntary sector. Hayek suggests that in order to buck this trend, we need to insist on restrictions on the scope of government activities, and to separate not only the finance and provision of those services done by the government, but also to challenge its monopoly on their provision.[25]

It may indeed be true that certain goods and services cannot effectively be provided by the market (given the current technological stage of development), but this should not be seen as a justification for coupling government finance and provision, let alone for giving the government monopoly status in provision. In particular, Hayek warns that claims to monopoly provision by the state are made not in order that citizens will be better served, but instead to enhance the powers of the government (see 1979, 56). As such, even when it has been established that the government should finance and produce a particular good or service, the claim of the state to be a monopoly provider— or the sole source of financial underwriting for such services—must be denied. The most harmful abuse that consumers face in their everyday life is not enduring high prices, but "the political coercion to make uneconomic use of resources" (1979, 59).

Competition, whether in the for-profit market setting or among nonprofit entities attempting to meet the needs of particular populations, ensures that actors will constantly be under pressure to respond more effectively in the production and distribution of the products under consideration. None of these processes will hit a hypothetical Pareto-Optimal outcome. Rather than compare markets, the nonprofit sector, and the state against an unattainable benchmark, however, we suggest that a positive theory ought to adopt a comparative-institutions analysis, one which addresses the dissemination of knowledge among participants as well as their incentives to act on that knowledge in ways to coordinate their plans further. We suggest, with Hayek, that monopoly privilege and the coercive power to tax in order to finance one's activities thwart the learning process and lead to ineffective use of resources and the inability to effectively meet the demands of the target population. Markets free of excessive government resources and intervention and an independent voluntary sector are better vehicles for promoting learning and social coordination.

Those who advocate a partnership between business and government on the one hand, and the voluntary sector and government on the other, as well as government taking on more and more responsibilities in our economic and social life, fail to recognize "that every step made in this direction means a transformation of more and more of the spontaneous order to [sic] society that serves the varying needs of the individuals, into an organization which can serve only a particular set of ends determined by the majority—or increasingly, since this organization is becoming far too complex to be understood by the voters, by the bureaucracy in whose hands the administration of those means is placed" (Hayek, 1979, 53).

We suggest, then, that the sort of "third party government" advocated by Salamon would distort the incentives for nonprofit innovation and weaken the ability of philanthropists and social entrepreneurs to fill in the gaps that might be left by for-profit firms before government bureaucracies expand to fill the supposed vacuum. A persistent lack of conceptual clarity cascades into a theoretical confusion over the nature of this sector, a confusion that might also color the way Salamon and others read the empirical data. Ultimately, government-nonprofit partnership will not invigorate the voluntary sector but instead will enervate it. Lohmann's approach provides a glimpse of the direction we might head, and we believe that further exploration of the field from an Austrian perspective will advance our understanding of the complex, fertile role of the voluntary sector in promoting human excellence, by offering the information necessary for both individual plan fulfillment and social cooperation.

NOTES

[1] See, for example, Salamon (1981, 1987, 1989, 1992, 1993, 1995, 1999, 2002a), Salamon and Abramson (1982), and Salamon and Anheier (1996a, 1996b). We will pay special attention to Salamon (1987), as it provides the clearest discussion of his theory of government-nonprofit partnership, one which continues to influence his most recent work.

[2] See Prychitko (1990, 2002a) for a criticism of the welfare state alternative, and Boettke (1993, 2001) for a criticism of post-communist policies in general.

[3] Recently, the methodology behind Salamon's empirical research has been strongly challenged by Smith (2000, 42-49).

[4] Salamon advances the normative claim that "cooperation between government and the nonprofit sector makes a great deal of sense both conceptually and practically. These two massive sets of institutions share many of the same basic objectives and have strengths and weaknesses that are mirror images of each other. Under the circumstances, the recent efforts [i.e., the Reagan reforms] to dismantle or significantly curtail this partnership seem singularly ill advised even if they are largely unintended. A more sensible approach would be to find ways to make this partnership truly work, not only for the 'partners' but also for those being served...The chapters presented in this book were originally written with this end in view...Now the challenge is to build on that start and set in motion a more basic effort to make government and the nonprofit sector not merely interconnected sets of institutions but true 'partners in public service'" (1995, 12-13). We applaud Salamon for at least making his ideological program explicit. Our own ideological vision differs, as we prefer both a robust and open market and nonprofit sector, and a substantial limitation on the powers of state compulsion.

[5] Salamon seems unaware of Boulding's work (1981), which is not founded on the market failure/government failure analysis. Boulding was a former professor of ours in the 1980s, and his work, particularly on knowledge transmission processes, fits nicely in the Austrian tradition.

[6] In a recent paper, Glaeser and Shleifer (1998) explore the question of when entrepreneurs may decide to enter the market as a for-profit or not-for-profit entity. They argue that this decision relates to the incentives that potential entrepreneurs face, such that under certain conditions even a self-inter-

ested entrepreneur will opt to enter as a not-for-profit entity.

[7] Salamon's terms can be confusing: aren't market organizations voluntarily formed and funded? So why distinguish between the "market sector" and the "voluntary sector"? What clarity does that add? In our view, the market sector would at least be seen as a subset of the voluntary sector. (At the same time, if one is to use these terms, why not label the state sector as the "compulsory sector"?) For now we shall stick with Salamon's terms: by "market sector," he means the traditional for-profit marketplace; by "voluntary sector" he means the panoply of nonprofit organizations; and by "government sector" he indeed means the state's legitimate monopoly on coercion. Finally, his term "third-party government" has nothing to do with political parties. It is, rather, merely his label for the institutional partnership between the federal government and other organizations, including nonprofits, one whereby the federal government "increasingly relies on a wide variety of "third parties"—states, cities, special districts, banks, hospitals, manufacturers, and others—to carry out its purposes" (Salamon 1981, 19). He also does not clearly distinguish nonprofit associations from not-for-profit firms. The importance of a clear distinction will be discussed in a later section.

[8] This is the notion of Pareto Optimality. Generally, in the Pareto Optimal market outcome, all prices are equilibrium prices, which reflect equalities between the marginal rates of substitution in consumption and the marginal rates of substitution in technical transformation. That is to say, different demanders have the same marginal values for a specific good, and different producers have the same marginal cost of producing that good, and those marginal values and marginal costs are equal to the (given) equilibrium market price of that good. For example, if the equilibrium price of a loaf of bread were $3.00, then consumers will purchase bread until they value the last ("marginal") loaf at $3.00, and bakers will produce up to the point that the last ("marginal") loaf produced costs $3.00. At this point, there is no longer room for mutually beneficial trade. Other things being constant, any given consumer would value *one more* loaf of bread less than $3.00; and any given baker could produce *one more* loaf of bread only at a cost higher than $3.00, so all bargaining possibilities have been fully exhausted.

[9] A negative externality or "spillover cost" occurs whenever a voluntary exchange between two parties negatively affects (reduces the utility, or wellbeing) of a third party not associated with the exchange. That party bears

some of the cost of the others' actions, without being compensated by a corresponding benefit. The outcome therefore fails to meet the Pareto-Optimal notion of efficiency: the traders gain, but others lose. In this sense, the market *overproduces* goods that generate negative externalities, because the trading parties fail to account for all the additional costs (the "social" marginal costs) of production. The counterpart to negative externality is, of course, positive externality, a kind of spillover benefit. Here, a third party enjoys a benefit of other traders' actions, without paying. Your landscaped and well-maintained lawn is a benefit to me across the street, although I don't pay a penny for the landscapers you hired. In principle, I, the free rider, would be willing to pay something to see your lawn in good shape, if not even nicer shape. With positive externalities, the market *underproduces*. More production would occur if free riders were to actually pay for the goods that they, too, enjoy. If they have no incentive to pay, potentially mutually beneficial exchange opportunities remain unexploited. This outcome, too, therefore fails to reach the Pareto-Optimal (what we shall simply call "efficient") level of output. A crucial part of all of this—known formally as the theory of welfare economics—is that *the concept of market failure makes sense only against the benchmark of the Pareto-Optimal, or fully efficient, ideal.* Pareto Optimality is the ideal against which standard economic theory evaluates market efficiency and market failure.

[10] See Boulding's "The Economics of Knowledge and the Knowledge of Economics" in Boulding (1966) and Hayek's "Economics and Knowledge" and "The Use of Knowledge in Society," in Hayek (1948, 33-56 and 77-91) for a general discussion of the assumptions of our knowledge in economic theory. On the particular issue of positive externalities and public goods, see Heyne, Boettke, and Prychitko (2003, 323-43) and Wagner (1996).

[11] Although he does occasionally use the term "optimal," as in "So long as sole reliance is placed on a system of voluntary contributions,...it is likely that the resources made available will be less than those society considers optimal" (1987, p. 45). Elsewhere he talks about the voluntary sector's "limited...ability to generate an adequate level of resources" (1987, 48). It is completely unclear precisely what "optimal" or "adequate" means in his new paradigm.

[12] Salamon regrets that, during the Reagan years, this structure began to lose its coveted place as the central organizing principle. See Salamon (1989, 1993).

At the same time, he has hope for other forms of nonprofit-state collaboration, as in the German corporatist model and the proposals set forth in the
U.K. Home Office Scrutiny Report (Salamon and Anheier 1996b, 121-22).

[13] Buchanan's point became conventional textbook material on the theory of
public goods, available long before Salamon embarked upon a new paradigm. Thus Jack Hirshleifer (1980, 542) writes,

> According to some welfare theorists, the various difficulties in private sup-
> ply of public goods dictate that they be "publicly" (i.e., governmentally)
> provided instead. Indeed, some have thought that the concept of public
> goods serves to define the proper scope of government: "Private goods"
> ought to be privately supplied, and "public goods" ought to be publicly
> supplied. But in fact we do observe private firms supplying public goods.
> Television broadcasting is the obvious example, but even lighthouse serv-
> ices have at times been privately provided. And on the other hand govern-
> ment agencies, while supplying public goods like national defense, are
> also in the business of producing a vast range of private goods. Among the
> many examples are electric power (TVA), irrigation water (the U.S. Bureau
> of Reclamation), insurance (Social Security), education (public schools),
> and of course postal services (the U.S. Mail).

[14] "The term *commons* as used in this book may refer to a club or membership
organization; social movement; political party, religious, artistic, scientific,
or athletic society; support group; network; conference of volunteers; or to
several other forms of what we think of as nonprofit or voluntary social
organization. As developed here, the term is an ideal type; it distills an
essential set of related characteristics that are seldom if ever empirically
observable in pure form. As an ideal type, we should expect to find in any
empirical commons evidence of altruistic motives and behavior; philanthropy; charity; patronage; various forms of donations and gift giving; and
programs that involve search, investigation, learning, and other ways of
expanding common endowments" (1992, 17-18). "Commons are not places
any more than are markets or states" (1992, 62).

[15] So far we have been using *nonprofit* as a catch-all term, as most of the literature does. But it is important to distinguish *nonprofit* organizations
from *not-for-profit* firms, which together compose the independent or voluntary sector, in the following way: nonprofit organizations are those that
do not typically charge a market price for their services; not-for-profit

organizations are firms that do charge a price for their services (like hospitals), and in principle can therefore calculate the expected and realized monetary "profit" or "residual" of their collective efforts. Cf. Lohmann's appeal to Anthony's distinction between Type A and Type B organizations (Lohmann (1991, 34). Lohmann's "commons" is that sector composed exclusively of nonprofit associations.

[16] See, for example, Boettke (1995a, 1995b), Prychitko (1995b, 1995c), and Boettke and Prychitko (1996). Lohmann's appeal to the role of producer cooperatives (1992, 143) also finds a sympathetic ear with one of us. See, for example, Prychitko and Vanek (1996).

[17] Alchian provides a strong critique of the maximization modeling even of for-profit activity in his classic 1950's paper, one which clearly had an early influence on Boulding (1958) and has inspired more recent work in evolutionary and new institutional economics.

[18] "Since productivity has always been associated with material wealth in the industrial society, many economists question the degree to which services actually generate wealth and are of value to society," laments Bruyn (1991, 324). "The issue, finally, as more and more social scientists are coming to realize, is finding a way to measure social wealth" (1991, 325). We shall suggest that such a measure will be impossible.

[19] See Kirzner's (1976) discussion of the evolution of economic theory, from the science of wealth (as found in Smith and the classicals) to the neoclassical science of economizing and maximizing (with Lionel Robbins, a subject of criticism by Lohmann [1991, 151]), to a more comprehensive theory of human action in general, in the work of Mises and the Austrian School.

[20] Smith:

> There is one sort of labour which adds to the value of the subject upon which it is bestowed: there is another which has no such effect. The former, as it produces a value, may be called productive; the latter, unproductive labour. Thus the labour of the manufacturer adds, generally, to the value of the materials which he works upon, that of his own maintenance, and of his master's profit. The labour of the menial servant, on the contrary, adds to the value of nothing. Though the manufacturer has his wages advanced to him by his master he, in reality, costs him no expense, the value of those wages being generally restored, together with a profit, in the improved value of the subject upon which his labour is bestowed.

But the maintenance of a menial servant never is restored. A man grows rich by employing a multitude of manufacturers: he grows poor, by maintaining a multitude of menial servants (1937, 314).

The labour of some of the most respectable order in the society is, like that of menial servants, unproductive of any value, and does not fix or realize itself in any permanent subject, or vendible commodity, which endures after that labour is past, and for which an equal quantity of labour could afterwards be procured (1937, 315).

Smith continues by citing "the whole army and navy,...churchmen, lawyers, physicians, men of letters of all kinds," as well as "players, buffoons, musicians, opera-singers, opera-dancers, etc."

[21] Now, there are important incentive issues that can be raised—specifically principal-agent issues—but that is separate from the calculation issue. Our remarks focus solely on whether or not a calculation problem exists in the philanthropic sector. These enterprises earn a profit, which can be calculated, but the profit is not owned by an entrepreneur. They might *make* profit, but the profit is not for any individual in particular.

[22] Mises (1981, 159):

Therefore it is absurd to want to apply the elements of this calculation to problems other than those confronting the individual actor [in the market process]. One may not extend them to *res extra commercium*. One may not attempt by means of them to include more than the sphere of the economic in the narrower sense. However, this is precisely what is attempted by those who undertake to ascertain the monetary value of human life, social institutions, national wealth, cultural ideals, or the like, or who enter upon highly sophisticated investigations to determine how exchange ratios of the relatively recent, not to mention the remote, past could be expressed in terms of "our money."

[23] We use the term "entrepreneur" only in the popular sense of being bold and venturesome here. If our argument is correct, nonprofit managers and foundation leaders *can't* undertake entrepreneurship in the strictly economic sense of profit-seeking. We wish to suggest only briefly here that they function instead like middlemen in the strict sense. They are "go-betweens," specialists who have a comparative advantage in reducing the transaction costs among donors and recipients, and it is this middleman function that helps coordinate the commons. This is a topic worthy of further research, which

one of the authors hopes to undertake in a separate paper.

[24] See Boettke and Rathbone (2002) for a discussion of the difficulties facing the philanthropic enterprise.

[25] As Hayek argues at one point, emphasizing the scale/scope issue, "In recent times it has been seriously maintained that the existing political institutions lead to an insufficient provision for the public sector. It is probably true that some of those services which the government ought to render are provided inadequately. But this does not mean that the aggregate of government expenditure is too small. It may well be true that having assumed too many tasks, government is neglecting some of the most important ones (1979, 53). Hayek does argue that we should worry about the scale of government, but the issue of scope may indeed be the more important. Government must be restricted to those tasks that it can accomplish with reasonable effectiveness, and strictly prohibited from engaging in those activities which it cannot accomplish in an efficient manner. The clarity of this delineation is clouded by the coercive power to levy taxes and to establish a monopoly in provision of the good or service under consideration.

REFERENCES

Alchian, Armen A. 1950. "Uncertainty, Evolution, and Economic Theory," *Journal of Political Economy* 58: 211-221. Reprinted in Alchian, *Economic Forces at Work*. Indianapolis: Liberty Fund, 1997.

Berger, Peter L., Richard John Neuhaus, and Michael Novak, eds. 1996. *To Empower People: From State to Civil Society*. Washington, D.C.: AEI Press.

Boettke, Peter. 1993. *Why Perestroika Failed*. New York: Routledge.

Boettke, Peter. 1995a. "Individuals and Institutions," in David L. Prychitko, ed. *Individuals, Institutions, Interpretations: Hermeneutics Applied to Economics*. Brookfield, VT: Avebury: 19-35.

Boettke, Peter. 1995b. "Interpretive Reasoning and the Study of Social Life," in David L. Prychitko, ed. *Individuals, Institutions, Interpretations: Hermeneutics Applied to Economics*. Brookfield, VT: Avebury: 59-80.

Boettke, Peter. 2001. *Calculation and Coordination*. New York: Routledge.

Boettke, Peter, and David L. Prychitko. 1996. "Mr. Boulding and the Austrians: Boulding's Contributions to Subjectivist Economics." In Laurence S. Moss, ed., *Joseph Schumpeter: Historian of Economics.* Perspectives on the History of Economic Thought Series. New York: Routledge: 250-59.

Boettke, Peter, and Ann Rathbone. 2002. "Civil Society, Social Entrepreneurship and Economic Calculation: Toward a Political Economy of the Philanthropic Enterprise." Working paper, Department of Economics, George Mason University.

Boulding, Kenneth E. 1958. *The Skills of the Economist.* Cleveland: Howard Allen.

Boulding, Kenneth E. 1966. "The Economics of Knowledge and the Knowledge of Economics." *American Economic Review,* 16 (May): 1-13.

Boulding, Kenneth E. 1969. "The Grants Economy," *Michigan Academician* (Winter). Reprinted in *Collected Papers of Kenneth Boulding: Vol. II: Economics.* Ed. Fred R. Glahe. Boulder, CO: Colorado Associated University Press, 1971: 177-85.

Boulding, Kenneth E. 1981. *A Preface to Grants Economics: The Economy of Love and Fear.* New York: Praeger.

Bruyn, Severyn T. 1991. *A Future for the American Economy: The Social Market* Stanford, CA: Stanford University Press.

Buchanan, James M. 1968. *The Demand and Supply of Public Goods.* Chicago: Rand McNally.

Buchanan, James M. 1975. *The Limits of Liberty.* Chicago: University of Chicago Press.

Cornuelle, Richard. 1965. *Reclaiming the American Dream.* New York: Random House.

Glaeser, Edward and Andrei Shleifer. 1998. "Not-for-Profit Entrepreneurs." National Bureau of Economic Research Working Paper 6810.

Hayek, F. A. 1948. *Individualism and Economic Order.* Chicago: University of Chicago Press.

Hayek, F. A. 1979. *Law, Legislation and Liberty: The Political Order of a Free People,* Vol. 3. Chicago: University of Chicago Press.

Heyne, Paul, Peter Boettke, and David Prychitko. 2002. *The Economic Way of Thinking.* 10th ed. Upper Saddle River, NJ: Prentice Hall.

Hirshleifer, Jack. 1980. *Price Theory and Applications.* 2nd ed. Englewood Cliffs, NJ: Prentice Hall.

Kirzner, Israel M. 1976. *The Economic Point of View: An Essay in the History of Economic Thought.* 2nd ed. Kansas City: Sheed and Ward.

Lohmann, Roger A. 1992. *The Commons: New Perspectives on Nonprofit Organizations and Voluntary Action.* San Francisco: Jossey-Bass.

Machlup, Fritz. 1958. "Equilibrium and Disequilibrium: Misplaced Concreteness and Disguised Politics." *Economic Journal*, LXVIII (March). Reprinted in Machlup, *Essays on Economic Semantics*. Englewood Cliffs, NJ: Prentice Hall, 1963: 43-72.

Mises, Ludwig von. 1933. *Epistemological Problems of Economics*. Trans. George Reisman. 1933; reprinted New York: New York University Press, 1981.

Mises, Ludwig von. 1966. *Human Action: A Treatise on Economics*. 3rd rev. ed. Chicago: Regnery.

Prychitko, David L. 1990. "The Welfare State: What is Left?." *Critical Review*, 4: 619-32.

Prychitko, David L. (ed.) 1995a. *Individuals, Institutions, Interpretations: Hermeneutics Applied to Economics*. Brookfield, VT: Avebury.

Prychitko, David L. 1995b. "Introduction: Why Hermeneutics?," in Prychitko (1995a): 1-5.

Prychitko, David L. 1995c. "Ludwig Lachmann and the Interpretive Turn in Economics: A Critical Inquiry into the Hermeneutics of the Plan," in Prychitko (1995a): 93-112.

Prychitko, David L. 2002a. "Does Market Socialism have a Future? From Lange and Lerner to Schumpeter and Stiglitz," in Prychitko (2002b): 156-67.

Prychitko, David L. 2002b. *Markets, Planning, and Democracy: Essays after the Collapse of Communism*. Northampton, MA: Edward Elgar.

Prychitko, David L., and Jaroslav Vanek (eds.). 1996. *Producer Cooperatives and Labor-Managed Systems Vol. I: Theory and Vol. II: Case Studies*, #62 in the International Library of Critical Writings in Economics, Mark Blaug, series editor. Brookfield, VT and Cheltenham, Glos.: Edward Elgar.

Salamon, Lester M. 1981. "Rethinking Public Management: Third-Party Government and the Changing Forms of Government Action," *Public Policy* 29 (3): 255-75. Reprinted in Salamon (1995): 17-32. Page numbers refer to 1995 reprint.

Salamon, Lester M. 1987. "Of Market Failure, Voluntary Failure, and Third-Party Government: Toward a Theory of Government-Nonprofit Relations in the Modern Welfare State," *Journal of Voluntary Action Research* 16 (1-2): 29-49. Reprinted in Salamon (1995): 33-49. Page numbers refer to 1995 reprint.

Salamon, Lester M. 1989. "The Voluntary Sector and the Future of the Welfare State," *Nonprofit and Voluntary Sector Quarterly* 18 (1): 11-24. Reprinted in Salamon (1995): 203-19. Page numbers refer to 1995 reprint.

Salamon, Lester M. 1992. "Social Services," in Charles Clotfelder (ed.), *Who Benefits from the Nonprofit Sector?* (Chicago: University of Chicago Press). Reprinted in Salamon (1995): 115-44, as "The Charitable Behavior of the Charitable Sector: The Case of Social Services." Page numbers refer to 1995 reprint.

Salamon, Lester M. 1993. "The Marketization of Welfare: Changing Nonprofit and For-Profit Roles in the American Welfare State," *Social Service Review* 67 (1): 16-39. Reprinted in Salamon (1995): 220-42. Page numbers refer to 1995 reprint.

Salamon, Lester M. 1995. *Partners in Public Service: Government-Nonprofit Relations in the Modern Welfare State.* Baltimore: Johns Hopkins University Press.

Salamon, Lester M. 1999. *America's Nonprofit Sector: A Primer.* Revised edition. New York: Foundation Center.

Salamon, Lester M. 2002a. "The Resilient Sector: The State of Nonprofit America," chapter 1 of Salamon (2002b), 3-61.

Salamon, Lester M., (ed.). 2002b. *The State of Nonprofit America.* Washington, D.C.: Brookings Institution Press.

Salamon, Lester M., and Alan J. Abramson. 1982. *The Federal Budget and The Nonprofit Sector.* Washington, D.C.: The Urban Institute Press.

Salamon, Lester M., and Helmut K. Anheier (eds.). 1996a. *Defining the Nonprofit Sector: A Cross-National Analysis.* Manchester: Manchester University Press.

Salamon, Lester M., and Helmut K. Anheier (eds.). 1996b. *The Emerging Nonprofit Sector: An Overview.* Manchester: Manchester University Press.

Smith, Adam. 1937 [1776]. *An Inquiry into the Nature and Causes of the Wealth of Nations* , edited by Edwin Cannan. New York: Modern Library.

Smith, David Horton. 2000. *Grassroots Associations.* Thousand Oaks, CA: Sage.

Stiglitz, Joseph E. 1994. *Whither Socialism?* Cambridge, MA: MIT Press.

Wagner, Richard E. 1996. *Economic Policy in a Liberal Democracy.* Brookfield, VT: Edward Elgar.

Weisbrod, Burton A. 1977. *The Voluntary Nonprofit Sector: Economic Theory and Economic Policy.* Lexington, MA: Lexington Press.

Weisbrod, Burton A. 1988. *The Nonprofit Economy.* Cambridge, MA: Harvard University Press.

COMMENT ON BOETTKE AND PRYCHITKO

Zoltan J. Acs
University of Baltimore

Peter J. Boettke and David L. Prychitko provide a valuable contribution to the debate on the relationship between the compulsory power of the state, the capitalist search for private monetary profit, and the spontaneous ordering of associations—the nonprofit sector. While there is general agreement across the political spectrum that the nonprofit sector plays an important role in American society, the exact nature of that role is in dispute.

Lester Salamon (1999) suggests that the nonprofit sector is not an independent sector but is an effective partner of the state and represents a viable "third party governance." Boettke and Prychitko (emphasis added) argue "that the sort of 'third party government' advocated by Salamon would distort the incentives for nonprofit innovation, *and weaken the ability of philanthropists and social entrepreneurs* to fill in the gaps that might be left by for-profit firms before government bureaucracies expand to fill the supposed vacuum." Before this Austrian interpretation of the nonprofit sector advocated by Boettke and Prychitko can be properly evaluated, we need to be a little clearer on the relationship between the nonprofit sector and economic development in general and the role of philanthropy in particular.

The word philanthropy literally means "love of mankind." Philanthropic acts manifest the generosity of the giver. In this comment, what we mean by philanthropy is giving money or its equivalent away to persons and institutions outside the family without a definite or immediate *quid pro quo* (Boulding, 1962).

Seeing a linkage between philanthropy and economic development is not new. In *Corruption and the Decline of Rome*, Ramsay MacMullen (1988) discusses how charitable foundations were partly responsible for the flourishing of Rome and how their decline coincided with the loss of the empire. The roots of American philanthropy can be found in England in the period from 1480 to 1660. By the close of the Elizabethan period, "it was generally agreed that all men must somehow be sustained at the level of subsistence" (Jordan, 1961: 401). Though the charitable organizations at the beginning of this period in England were centered around religion and the role of the Church, by the close of the sixteenth century, religious charities comprised only 7 percent of all charities (Jordan, 1961: 402).

Acs, Zoltan. 2004. Comment on Boettke and Prychitko. *Conversations on Philanthropy I*: 41-44.
ISSN 1552-9592 © 2004 DonorsTrust.

How is this philanthropic behavior explained? According to Jordan, there was the partly religious and partly secular sensitivity to human pain and suffering in sixteenth-century England. Doubtless, another important motivating factor was Calvinism, which taught that "the rich man is a trustee for wealth which he disposes for benefit of mankind, as a steward who lies under direct obligation to do Christ's will" (Jordan, 1961: 406-7).

Beginning with the Puritans, who regarded excessive profit-making as both a crime and a sin (and punished it accordingly), there is a long history of Americans who have questioned the right of people to become rich. In view of the popular prejudice against ostentatious enjoyment of riches, the luxury of doing good was almost the only extravagance the American rich of the first half of the nineteenth century could indulge in with good conscience (Tocqueville, 1966 (1835): 40).

Andrew Carnegie exemplified the ideal Calvinist. Carnegie put philanthropy at the heart of his "gospel of wealth." For Carnegie, the question was not only, "How to gain wealth?" but also, importantly, "What to do with it?" *The Gospel of Wealth* suggested that millionaires, instead of bequeathing vast fortunes to heirs or making benevolent grants by will, should administer their wealth as a public trust during life (Carnegie, 1889). Both Carnegie (at the time) and Jordan (as a historian) suggest that a key motive for philanthropy is social order and harmony.

Philanthropy remained part of an implicit social contract stipulating that wealth beyond a certain point should revert to society. Individuals are free to accumulate wealth, but the wealth must be invested back into society to expand opportunity. Therefore, much of the new wealth created historically has been given back to the community to build up the great social institutions *that have a positive feedback on future economic development* (Chernow, 1999).

The American model of entrepreneurship and philanthropy in the nineteenth century was followed by a period of progressivism (increasing role of government) in the early years of the twentieth century. Though the period of the 1920s was one of technological change and prosperity, underlying economic problems resulted in the collapse of the world economy into the Great Depression of the 1930s. This period, together with that of World War II, changed the role of the government and the philanthropic activities of the entrepreneur. It is not our point here to argue that the role of philanthropy was to provide social welfare—such as health insurance, social security, and unemployment insurance. Indeed, the rise of the state in the twentieth century was in some ways a rise of social welfare, provided by government.

This function of social welfare, however, is distinct from the pure function of philanthropy that arises from issues of what an individual should do with personal wealth. The rise of the welfare state, with its high marginal taxes, high inheritance taxes, antitrust laws, and the abolition of private property in some societies, tried to eliminate the role of private wealth altogether. In fact, in a socialist state the only role for philanthropy might be religious giving.

What is interesting is that in the United States the rise of the welfare state did not coincide with a decline in philanthropy. In fact, according to a study by the National Bureau of Economic Research (Dickinson, 1970), total private domestic philanthropy as a percentage of U.S. Gross National Product between 1929 and 1959 increased from 1.7 percent to 2.3 percent. This figure is not significantly different from the 2.5 percent that Americans contributed to philanthropic causes in 2003. Why did Americans continue to fund philanthropy at at a fairly constant level even as the federal government stepped into the business of social welfare?

One answer was suggested by Soloman Fabricant, and has been echoed by many others (Dickinson, 1970: 8):

...in this broad sense philanthropy is a necessary condition of social existence, and the extent to which it is developed influences an economy's productiveness. For decent conduct pays large returns to society as a whole, partly in the form of a higher level of national income than would otherwise be possible. Underdeveloped countries are learning that, despite their hurry to reach desired levels of economic efficiency, time must be taken to develop the kind of business ethics, respect for the law, and treatment of strangers that keep a modern industrial society productive. Widening of the concepts of family loyalty and tribal brotherhood to include love of man "in general" is a necessary step in the process of economic development.

The key issue, therefore, in the debate on the role of the nonprofit sector is the *voluntary* nature of the contribution of the donor. As Boettke and Prychitko point out in Salamon's model "many nonprofits often bypass the responsibility of persuasion and voluntary exchange and instead seek support from the state. In this regard, to accept Salamon's advocacy of third-party government, which in effect seeks to legitimate nonprofit firms as arms of state action, would further weaken the effectiveness of nonprofit organizations to promote economic development by encouraging them to engage more in political rent-seeking than in marketplace persuasion."

What is unique about America is not that it has "an intricate 'mixed economy' that blends public and private action in ways that few people truly understand" (Salamon, 1999), but that a crucial component of American economic, political, and social stability rests on the role of philanthropy in American society. The fulcrum of this relationship is between the *private* and the *nonprofit* sectors. What differentiates American capitalism from all other forms of capitalism is its historical focus on both the creation of wealth (entrepreneurship) and the reconstitution of wealth (philanthropy) through an independent nonprofit sector (Acs and Phillips, 2002).

REFERENCES

Acs, Zoltan J. and Ronnie, J. Phillips. 2002. "Entrepreneurship and Philanthropy in American Capitalism," *Small Business Economics*, 19, 189-204.

Boulding, Kenneth. 1962. "Notes on a Theory of Philanthropy," in Frank G. Dickinson, ed., *Philanthropy and Public Policy*. Boston: NBER, 57-72.

Bremner, Robert, H. 1960. *American Philanthropy*. Chicago: University of Chicago Press.

Carnegie, Andrew. 1889. "Wealth," *North American Review*, (June).

Chernow, Ron. 1999. *Titan: The Life of John D. Rockefeller Sr.* New York: Vintage.

Dickinson, Frank, G. 1970. *The Changing Position of Philanthropy in the American Economy*. National Bureau of Economic Research, Distributed by Columbia University Press, New York.

Jordan, W. K. 1961. "The English Background of Modern Philanthropy." *The American Historical Review* 66 (2), 401-408.

MacMullen, Ramsay. 1998. *Corruption and the Decline of Rome*. New Haven: Yale University Press.

Salamon, Lester M. 1999. *America's Nonprofit Sector: A Primer*, 2nd ed. New York: The Foundation Center.

Tocqueville, Alexis de. 1966 (1835). *Democracy in America*. New York: Harper and Row.

COMMENT ON BOETTKE AND PRYCHITKO

Emily Chamlee-Wright
Beloit College

By challenging the condition of Pareto Optimality as the benchmark against which the voluntary sector is compared, Boettke and Prychitko make an important correction in the literature on the philanthropic process. In addition, their analysis of the relationship between the state and the voluntary sector sends a chilling warning. State funding of nonprofit organizations may ultimately erode the voluntary sector's ability to serve as a check on government power. Further, I agree with the authors that Austrian economics has much to contribute to our understanding of the philanthropic process, and it is on this point that I wish to devote the substance of my commentary.

Specifically, I want to challenge the starkness with which Boettke and Prychitko draw the distinction between profit-seeking firms and nonprofit organizations. By emphasizing the theme of calculation within the Austrian intellectual tradition, the authors focus too little on the Austrian themes of non-price discovery and local knowledge. By developing these themes— themes that both Boettke and Prychitko emphasize elsewhere—I argue that we would go further in advancing our understanding of philanthropic processes.[1]

Boettke and Prychitko direct our attention to the Austrian school's understanding of economic calculation in order to "contribute to the development of an alternative theory of nonprofits." Nonprofit organizations, the authors argue, are incapable of engaging in economic calculation. Following Mises' argument regarding the impossibility of rational calculation in the context of a centrally planned economy, Boettke and Prychitko carefully draw the distinction between calculation and measurement:

> [Calculation] is not merely measurement as in some input/output flow chart. After all, Soviet planners could measure how much land, labor, fertilizer, tractors, and so on it took to produce a ton of wheat on the collective farms. But they couldn't calculate the added value of that effort to determine whether they had used those resources efficiently and productively. Lacking market-generated prices, they had no way of solving, with Mises, "the task of allocating [scarce resources] to those employments in which they can render the best service" (1966, p. 207). They couldn't

Chamlee-Wright, Emily. 2004. Comment on Boettke and Prychitko. *Conversations on Philanthropy I:* 45-51. ISSN 1552-9592 © 2004 DonorsTrust.

determine whether or not their production plans were worth the cost, i.e., whether they generated a positive *net improvement* in wealth...[Central planners] lack the knowledge to plan the economy successfully because they lack the ability to calculate.

Economic calculation affords entrepreneurs the ability to check their expectations against the realized monetary net return for their efforts, and as such provides an essential and meaningful set of signals for how the entrepreneur might revise plans and set a course for future action.

It is not necessary for the entrepreneur to retain the profits earned from an enterprise in order to engage in economic calculation, the authors argue. Not-for-profit organizations, because they charge for their services, are capable of calculating the residual above and beyond the costs of providing those services. Nonprofit organizations, on the other hand, are in an entirely different situation. Because they do not charge for their services, they have no way of engaging in economic calculation. Certainly a nonprofit can make judicious use of monetary prices when counting up its costs, but there is no way to determine through economic calculation whether society is, on net, better off for their efforts.

At this point in the paper, it sounds as though the authors are suggesting that nonprofit organizations are akin to state enterprises in a soviet economy, likely to generate pronounced inefficiencies. But surprisingly, Boettke and Prychitko spare nonprofits from this condemnation. The authors liken decision-making in the nonprofit sector to decision-making within the family, or a decision that preserves a historical landmark, or a piece of great, though non-vendible art. When making decisions in contexts such as these, we know that our "specific goals and efforts are worthwhile," and for this reason, the nonprofit sector is not systematically prone to failure in efficiency terms.

But this raises the question: *How* do we know this? How do we assess the worthiness of contributing resources to non-vendible objects and services? According to Mises, we know their worthiness directly:

> Those things that do not enter into the items of accountancy and calculation are either ends or goods of the first order. No calculation is required to acknowledge them fully and make due allowance to them. All that acting man needs in order to make his choice is to contrast them with the total amount of costs their acquisition or preservation requires. (Mises 1966: 215, cited in Boettke & Prychitko).

On one level, this makes sense. If Bill and Melinda Gates value finding a cure for AIDS and other infectious diseases enough to spend $1.2 billion on the effort, they will know directly whether such expenditures are worthwhile. Donors in this sense are like consumers—they are the ultimate arbiter of what their philanthropic ventures are worth to them. The Gates family may experience "buyer's remorse" if the pace of achievement proves too slow for their liking, but the decision itself was nothing less than rational. Further, as Boettke and Prychitko argue, the philanthropic process provides a way for donors like the Gates family to coordinate their plans with the medical research community, and, therefore, it is not systematically prone to failure in terms of efficiency.

But the decision to give to this or that cause represents only one level of the decision-making process in the nonprofit environment. How best to achieve the goals of a nonprofit organization is far more complex than donors directly assessing whether their contributions are worthwhile to them personally. The complexities of decision-making within the operations of a typical nonprofit are significant enough to throw open the door once again to the question of whether the voluntary sector is systematically prone to failure.

An active question within the economic development literature, for example, is whether microfinance organizations in the developing world ought to charge a fee for services such as business training, literacy courses, marketing courses, and the like, if for no other reason than to provide organization managers the meaningful feedback they need to know whether they are offering the right mix of services (see Chamlee-Wright, forthcoming).[2]

Even when we consider Boettke and Prychitko's own example of the "family as nonprofit," the decision-making process seems far more complex than the authors suggest. Boettke and Prychitko offer the following example to show how families, like so many other nonprofit organizations, are able to engage in rational decision-making despite their inability to engage in economic calculation: "Although [parents] cannot *calculate* the value added of their efforts, they can determine whether their specific goals and efforts are worthwhile." Presumably, parents are able to determine the worthiness of their decisions because they know directly what value they attach to their family's well-being.

But is it really that simple? In some cases it may be. The parents ask themselves, "Is correcting my child's overbite worth the $4,000 in orthodontic care? Yes. Is my child's desire to wear the latest tennis shoe fashion worth the $250 price tag? No." But most of the decision-making that takes place in this nonprofit we call the family is far more complex. We may know directly *that* we value our family's well being, but *how* exactly to achieve our goals is fraught with uncertainty. To instill a sense of confidence in our children, do we encourage them to try a variety of different activities or do we encourage the development of a single talent? Do we choose a home in the city, with all the cultural amenities it has to offer, or do we raise our children in the country where the pace of life is more relaxed? Do we pay for private piano lessons or take a family vacation instead? I agree with Boettke and Prychitko that in this context economic calculation is impossible. But the question of whether rational choice is possible in this non-calculative environment is not resolved simply by saying that we know the worthiness of our decisions directly. Much of the decision-making that takes place in the context of a nonprofit involves the weighing of two (or perhaps many more) alternative courses of action, each of which could be imagined to meet the goals of the organization but none presenting itself as clearly the best alternative a priori. Directors of nonprofits must test their expectations in a process of trial and error. Though discovery will not take the form of economic calculation, they will nonetheless discover.

The problem here is that Boettke and Prychitko draw too stark a distinction between organizations that calculate and those that do not:

[T]here is either calculation or there isn't. There are no "proxies for calculation"—issues of trust, reputation, satisfaction, and so on might serve as effective guides to action, but they cannot serve as sources for calculation itself...Without a priced service, the agents of nonprofit organizations and their donors might engage in "pseudo-calculation," but let's understand that that really means no calculation.

This characterization suggests that economic calculation in the market context is something more than a mere "guide to action." I don't question whether monetary profits and losses are central to the learning process in the market, but the difference between economic calculation and other guides to action is one of degree, not of kind. Market prices and net monetary returns are not "marching orders." Profits tell the entrepreneur that she or he is doing *something* right, but profits do not necessarily signal whether some alternative plan might have generated even more profits. Losses certainly signal the entrepreneur that *something* is wrong, but just what the entrepreneur is supposed to do in response to these losses is a complex interpretive challenge (Ebeling 1986: 45). Indeed, profits and losses are essential guides to action, but they are *guides*, not logical directives. As all the possible courses of action and their corresponding outcomes are never laid out before market participants, entre-preneurial decision-making is a process of discovery, not logical deduction (O'Driscoll & Rizzo 1996: 103; see also Hayek 1948). Though monetary calcu-lation is central to market discovery, nonmonetary discovery also takes place as entrepreneurs execute and revise their plans. This dimension of learning within the market seems to be lost in the current discussion.

The authors' stark distinction between calculating and non-calculating organizations also misrepresents the nature of the discovery process that takes place in the voluntary sector. As Boettke and Prychitko argue, in the absence of a priced output, nonprofits cannot engage in economic calculation. Yet, as I have argued, many of the most important choices facing nonprofits are com-plex enough that decision makers will not be able to discern directly the wor-thiness of any particular course of action. Does this mean that nonprofit organ-izations are akin to state-owned enterprises in a soviet-type economy, such that if efforts exerted in the nonprofit sector add (on net) value to society, it will only be by accident?

In that nonprofits cannot rely upon economic calculation, the answer seems to depend on whether directors of nonprofits have access to and can make use of alternative guides to action. Casual observation seems to suggest that many nonprofits have access to a rich source of local knowledge that serves as a meaningful guide to action. A mother looks for cues that her son's involvement in high school sports is contributing to or inhibiting the develop-ment of other life skills. The director of a domestic violence center tries to understand the particular reasons some clients return to their abusive spouse and others do not. She may adjust the center's programs in response, and watch to see whether the changes make a difference. Parents and directors of nonprofits may avail themselves of the latest scholarly literature that pertains to their situation, but ultimately it is access to this local (often tacit) knowl-edge that offers the chance of successful planning and plan revision.

Surely, the guidance such nonmonetary signals provide will not be as clear as the guidance offered by profit and loss calculations, but when we consider that even profit-seeking entrepreneurs need to cultivate nonmonetary guides to action in order to make sense of profit and loss signals, we see that the dis-tance between nonprofit organizations and profit-seeking firms may not be as great as the calculating/non-calculating distinction suggests. A clear distinction *does* exist, however, between profit-seeking firms—which can make use of both economic calculation and relevant local knowledge—and state-owned enterprises, which are systematically incapable of doing either (see Lavoie 1995). With regard to nonprofits, the question seems to be whether they are capable of cultivating enough relevant local knowledge to serve as an effective guide to action. There is no guarantee that any one particular organization will be able to do this, but there is no systematic reason why we would expect sector-wide failure in this regard, either.

An organization's size, its scope of operations, and its proximity to the people it aims to serve are all potentially important factors in determining its access to relevant local knowledge. But ultimately it is the degree of connectedness, no matter how that might be achieved, that allows the decision maker in the organization to "dwell" in the mind of a person receiving their services. This potential for local knowledge to serve as a cognitive guide in the trial and error process requires further development on both the theoretical and empirical levels of research.

Though the Austrian understanding of economic calculation is indeed an important concept, if we are to understand better the philanthropic process, the Austrian concepts of nonmonetary discovery and the cultivation of local knowledge are equally relevant, if not more so. The inability to engage in economic calculation extends to all nonprofits and therefore does not offer a way to understand why some nonprofits are more successful in achieving their stated goals than others. Nonprofit organizations do differ, however, with regard to their ability to engage in discovery processes of trial and error, and they differ in their access to and ability to make use of relevant local knowledge. Understanding the ways in which nonprofits cultivate and make use of nonprice guides to action may go a long way in helping us to understand differences in performance among nonprofit organizations.

NOTES

[1] See, for example, Prychitko's edited volume *Individuals, Institutions, Interpretations: Hermeneutics Applied to Economics*, and Boettke's contribution "Interpretive Reasoning and the Study of Social Life" in the same volume.

[2] The nonprofit sector may also suffer from perverse incentives as managers

are not rewarded or punished according to the monetary return their decisions earn for the organization, and this can of course lead to significant principal/agents problems as Boettke and Prychitko point out. The current discussion, however, rests on issues of whether nonprofit managers have access to the *knowledge* they require to make rational decisions in the philanthropic process, an issue that remains even if we assume that the interests of the manager match up perfectly with the stated goals of the organization.

REFERENCES

Boettke, Peter. 1995. "Interpretive Reasoning and the Study of Social Life," in Prychitko (ed.) (1995): 59-80.

Chamlee-Wright, Emily. Forthcoming. "Entrepreneurial Response to Bottom-up Development Strategies in Zimbabwe," *The Review of Austrian Economics.*

Ebeling, Richard. 1986. "Toward a Hermeneutical Economics: Expectations, Prices, and the Role of Interpretation in a Theory of the Market Process." In Kirzner, I. (ed.) *Subjectivism, Intelligibility, and Economic Understanding.* New York: New York University Press.

Hayek, F. A. 1948. "The Use of Knowledge in Society," in *Individualism and Economic Order.* Chicago: University of Chicago Press.

O'Driscoll, Gerald and Rizzo, Mario. 1996. *The Economics of Time and Ignorance.* London: Routledge.

Lavoie, Don. 1995. "The Market as a Procedure for the Discovery and Conveyance of Inarticulate Knowledge," in Prychitko (ed.) (1995): 115-37.

Mises, Ludwig von. 1966 *Human Action.* Chicago: Contemporary Books.

Prychitko, David (ed.). 1995. *Individuals, Institutions, Interpretations: Hermeneutics Applied to Economics.* Brookfield, VT: Avebury.

COMMENT ON BOETTKE AND PRYCHITKO

Roger Lohmann
West Virginia University

I appreciate very much the opportunity to provide written reaction to the Boettke-Prychitko paper "Is an Independent Nonprofit Sector Prone to Failure?" It is one of the most basic rewards of intellectual effort in the crowded contemporary marketplace of ideas to have one's ideas noticed. Today's scholarly world of surplus production of papers, articles, and books produces something of a hierarchy of notice: to have one's work noticed at all is good and more rare than one might otherwise anticipate; to provoke a reaction is even better, and when that reaction is both critically ambitious and favorable, one has perhaps the best reward possible.

In this brief commentary I would like to offer a few additional thoughts in response to specific comments by Boettke and Prychitko on the economic perspective of my book *The Commons*. But first, a bit of background may be appropriate. The book itself is an effort to contribute to a unified theory of nonprofit organization, voluntary action, and philanthropy (Lohmann, 1992). It grew out of an earlier paper entitled "And Lettuce is Nonanimal: Toward An Economics of Voluntary Action" (Lohmann, 1989). The task of theory-building in this area is, inherently, an interdisciplinary one crossing many intellectual limits and boundaries. My principal interest in this topic is summed up well by Richard Cornuelle's marvelous—and too much ignored—concept of an *independent* sector. As Boettke and Prychitko correctly note, I was (and am) as concerned with the independence of a realm for nonprofit organization, voluntary action, and philanthropy from the marketplace and the household as from the state.

There are many powerful and fundamental disagreements over the coercive powers of the state, the productivity of the marketplace, and the penumbra of privacy for households and families. Regardless of how extensive or limited a role one holds out for states, markets, and households, however, simple logic dictates the existence of an additional social space devoted to activities other than governing, buying and selling, personal intimacy, and procreation and the raising of children.

It is that space, the zone associated by the ancients with such terms as *koinonia, philia, benefice, waqf,* and *kanjin,* to which I was seeking to give name and shape in *The Commons*. The task as I construe it is a fundamentally multidisciplinary one, invoking insights from at least two dozen different

Lohmann, Roger. 2004. Comment on Boettke and Prychitko. *Conversations on Philanthropy* I: 52-58. SSN 1552-9592 © 2004 DonorsTrust.

arts, sciences, disciplines, and professions, including art history as well as economics. The sheer scope of the topic so conceived gives us reason to take seriously Boettke and Prychitko's invocation of Ludwig von Mises' praxeology. I might be so bold as to suggest that my purpose in *The Commons* was praxeological even before I became aware of the term itself.

Some of the readers of this conversation are committed to the central importance of the idea of philanthropy, for example, with significantly less interest in questions of nonprofit organization or voluntary action. I know from my experience as editor of *Nonprofit Management and Leadership* that the Salamon-Weisbrod "failure theory" perspective—however faulty Boettke and Prychitko find it to be in their paper—is very widely shared. This is especially the case among those researchers, scholars, and students of nonprofit management who find the growth of public purchase of services contracting and the rise of the QUANGO (quasi-nongovernmental organization) to be the centrally important trend of interest within this whole broad area. In part, I took some of the positions I did in the book precisely to refute *the* centrality of this development. My view remains that in some primary, definitional sense, voluntary action and philanthropy in an independent sector are constitutive and paradigmatic of this whole range of activity, even as the QUANGO is largely a matter of marginal and momentary interest.

Thus, I did not in *The Commons* (and still do not) take the rise of a highly visible "sector" of publicly dependent, tax-exempt enterprises to be a development of much intrinsic interest for nonprofit organization, voluntary action, and philanthropy *theory*. In my view, it is a momentary transitioning for entirely political reasons away from the "reluctant welfare state" of the New Deal and Great Society toward something else—what else is not yet altogether clear. In the meantime, public supplicants and retainers are an old and relatively well-understood phenomenon, and the fact that some of them act in the name of organizations and fashion themselves as "nonprofit managers," "public health" or "social work professionals," "community arts supporters," or by some other *nom de guerre* does not in itself lend great theoretical weight to claims that their behavior represents something entirely new and unprecedented.

My claim in the book was rather that contemporary nonprofit, voluntary, and philanthropic developments in the United States were (and are) some of the latest chapters in a much older and more universal set of occurrences leading back through the early Middle Ages in Europe and as far afield as the efforts of the Buddhist emperor-turned-philanthropist Ashoka. The fact that nonmarket, nongovernmental voluntary action and philanthropy have existed for so long and attracted so little attention by social philosophers and theorists (with a few notable exceptions like Tocqueville) is as sad as it is truly remarkable.

With that bit of background in mind, let us turn to a couple of additional points raised in the Boettke and Prychitko paper. Perhaps the crucial assessment of the economics offered in *The Commons* was the following:

> Although some of Lohmann's criticisms are generally correct in spirit, his proposed revisions to mainstream economic analysis (such as his attempt to rectify the classical distinction between "productive" and "unproductive" labor) are unfortunate and can be better developed using the insights of Austrian economic theory."

Let me end all suspense here by noting that I have no quarrel with the thrust of this conclusion. I very much appreciate (and agree with) the sympathetic reading Boettke and Prychitko give to the economic portions of my work, published more than a decade ago, and I now believe their correction of my apparent misstep over the Smithian productive/unproductive labor point to be an accurate one. I have no wish to call for a renaissance of classical economics!

The question now for all of us, however, is what are the next steps in advancing a theoretical understanding of the economics of philanthropy? Boettke and Prychitko make a strong (although somewhat preliminary and sketchy) case for an Austrian economics, based on the work of Mises and his praxeology in particular, that ought to be of interest to nonprofit economists and all others (especially noneconomists like myself) interested in philanthropology. Their case for a praxeology becomes even stronger when one moves beyond the single lens of economic theory and acknowledges the essentially multidisciplinary nature of the task. Of course, someone needs to attend—as they do—to the economics of the matter; but others also need to attend—as I sought to do—to the relation between those economics and the social, political, cultural, historical, spiritual, and other aspects of philanthropy. If they do not, we can expect the same old familiar social-science muddles, with economists concluding it really is an economic phenomenon, sociologists that it is a social matter, anthropologists that culture is the key, and each of the assorted representatives of professional, quasi-professional, and other third-sector service providers asserting primacies of their own. In other words, the theory of the third sector will be a varied expression of the very play of narrow self-interests that Boettke and Prychitko and I seek to void. They correctly capture my original intent quite accurately in the following: "Lohmann criticizes the failure project for apparently grafting a theory of narrow self-interest and profit-seeking onto a social domain that substantially differs from market activity." A bit later they add, "Lohmann stresses—correctly in our view—that human action in general is not exclusively of the narrowly self-interested variety." These are fundamentally correct readings not only of my words but also of my intentions.

One of the most interesting points for me in the Boettke and Prychitko paper, as those who have read chapter 1 of *The Commons* will recognize, were their comments in defense of economic language. They note that noneconomists often adopt and use terms like *public goods, market failure*, and *government failure* "loosely, and erroneously, for the terms have specific meanings." If anything, they understate the matter in their paper. Merely to use terms of art differently than their originators is, of course, one of the most common practices in social science and social theory language use. That in itself is not problematic. The problem arises, as Boettke and Prychitko note, when such terms have very specific meanings and exist within a closely reasoned body of existing theory and the misuses—whether deliberate or not—tend to modify, amend, or in some cases even nullify the original significance of the term. I was convinced when I wrote *The Commons*, as Boettke and Prychitko note, that something like this has happened in the case of these three terms (and others).

Boettke and Prychitko make an even stronger and clearer case than I that this is so. Although they focus this critique on Salamon's writings in particular, I see it more as a general problem of what we might term the nonprofit paradigm—a kind of subculture of understandings (and misunderstandings) that has arisen among a great many writers on nonprofit matters. No one person is solely responsible for the paradigm or for the resulting econobabble it has produced; it is a cousin in many respects of "pop" psychology, perhaps at a slightly higher educational level, being limited as yet to a largely postgraduate audience. Nevertheless, it results from a culture very tolerant of slipshod usage.

Within this scholarly and practical subculture, these three terms as well as others like *efficiency, productivity*, and *output* have evolved additional meanings that simply overwhelm the more precise and careful theoretical understandings of economists and all those seeking to attend to careful usage. In this common parlance, *public goods* become simply any products and services that are purveyed by governments or paid for by tax revenues. Such a usage is entirely descriptive and completely voids any possible normative economic connotations

VOLUME 1. 2004. . . 55

of the more careful, original usage. Another, which I deal with in the book and elsewhere, is the sleight-of-hand substitution (often via concepts of "systems" theory) through which the engineering concept of efficiency as the ratio of input and output replaces the economic concept. This sets up the familiar *reductio ad absurdum* in which that which never happens is always more efficient than anything that does, and the very real practical situation of the present in which *any* cost reduction can be deemed an improvement in efficiency.

Market failure is likewise often removed from the exact economic context noted by Boettke and Prychitko, and is used as a two-way, all-purpose rationale for nonprofit activity: if goods are provided by some nonprofits somewhere, it must be because a market for them has failed to materialize. If a government subsidy for nonprofits exists, it is similarly treated as evidence of a market failure. In both of these cases, we are dealing more with the sociopolitical dynamics of mission definition and goal displacement than with anything recognizably economic.

This is, of course, most definitely not a process limited to economics or even to philanthropology. The abuse of economic terms in such cases is often largely rhetorical: to harness the power and legitimacy of economic "science" to justify and rationalize noneconomic matters. Economists such as Boettke and Prychitko have every right to insist upon the proper use of economic theory; noneconomists, however, should be equally concerned. Robert Payton's definition of philanthropy as *private action for the public good*, a formulation originally set forth along lines reminiscent of Cornuelle's independent sector, has come in for similar rough treatment, as have such terms as *civil society, social entrepreneurship*, and the current hands-down favorite for misuse, *social capital*. One of the things I was attempting in *The Commons* was the rather arduous challenge of a noneconomist who strives to use those terms more or less correctly. That I have apparently done so, with the exception noted above, is most gratifying.

One point where I might beg to differ slightly with Boettke and Prychitko is over my intent in using the notion of scarcity. They say that I slip a bit with the concept of surplus. This is less a disagreement over economic meanings than about additional implications. I have no quarrel with their interpretation of the economists' concept of economic scarcity; it is, as they note, a matter of epistemological positioning rather than empirical fact: life is indeed short, and resources are limited; that choices must be made is simply reality.

My point in *The Commons* was rather a different one, and perhaps by using the economic terms too loosely, I have obscured it: it strikes me still that just as scarcity in the economic sense exists and must be recognized and dealt with, it is also the case that some rudimentary measure of what I termed the assumption of affluence is necessarily associated with all philanthropic acts. Making any gift requires first having something of value to give, and charitable volunteering or engaging in association with others requires having leisure time available. Moreover, the potential reductionism of the theory of subjective choice is mitigated in this instance by the fact that for something to be truly of value it must be important to both giver and recipient. This makes the determination of philanthropic value inherently a social, rather than a purely individual, judgment. If one has something deemed valuable (advice, let's say) to give, and no one wishes to receive it, it is not valuable in a philanthropic sense. In this way, the Austrian School points up a fundamental limit on having "a wealth of experience."

This is all part of what I meant to denote by the assumption of affluence. I agree that it has nothing whatsoever to do with material wealth, even though my examples did, except insofar as material wealth is something both giver and recipient prize. Assuming affluence as a precondition of philanthropic action in this way need not be in any respect inconsistent with the economic concept of scarcity. Indeed, the choice, for example, of whether to invite a friend to accompany you as your guest to a sporting event or to join you in working the noon shift at a soup kitchen is a good expression of the principle of scarcity in operation and also of the assumption of affluence. Economic scarcity dictates that you cannot do both; the interpersonal nature of the determination of philanthropic value dictates that both of you prefer one over the other, and the principle of affluence dictates that the choice makes no sense if the time is not free. "Sorry, but I have to work then" is not simply stating another alternative in the choice; it nullifies the gift situation.

I also appreciate and concur with the authors' modest appraisal of the role of the theory of value in the overall scheme of philanthropology: "the subjective theory of value cannot help produce overall efficient allocation of philanthropic resources (or of tax-generated resources for welfare). Here, more broad accomplishment of plan fulfillment must suffice in the absence of some more comprehensive yet undefinable and unattainable standard of social optimality."

In concluding, Boettke and Prychitko write, "With Lohmann, we believe that the nonprofit sector is viable and, we should add, productive." They then refer back to the unproductive-labor issue already dealt with above, about which I have nothing further to add. They continue: "This leads us back to the normative issue of whether the commons should be a largely independent sector or whether its 'partnership' with the state is a promising development."

Setting aside current political and ideological questions, there are several things of importance for me in this statement. First, and most importantly perhaps, the recognition on purely economic grounds of genuine economic viability and productivity of nonprofit, voluntary, and philanthropic activity are of the greatest importance. Secondly, Boettke and Prychitko are among the few reviewers and critics of The Commons to recognize the centrality of its normative as well as its empirical aspirations. My overall project was not merely to describe and explain, but also to affirm and value nonprofit, voluntary, and philanthropic activity.

I would state the final issue they raise slightly differently, even while agreeing that "a largely independent sector" is a type worth pursuing. For me, the "partnership" between nonprofit corporations and the political state is not a phenomenon that properly belongs within the domain of a nonprofit sector at all, and is most assuredly not a characteristic or definitive activity of a third sector in any meaningful sense. It is, at best, a marginal activity occurring in some vague atheoretical borderland between the third sector and the state, and more probably an activity that belongs entirely within the latter. Close observation of many such organizations over a number of years forces me to the conclusion that those nonprofit organizations that become "partners" of government necessarily also become agents of government; to believe otherwise, that they retain some fundamental independence, is merely wishful thinking. "Partners" they may be, but it is definitely a junior partnership in the most meaningful sense. I agree that deciding whether or not this is a promising development is a question that deserves our closest scrutiny. To do so, however, is a separate issue from the equally important matter of the nature and functioning of a truly independent sector or commons.

REFERENCES

Lohmann, R. A. 1989. "And Lettuce is Non-Animal: Toward a Positive Economics of Nonprofit Action." *Nonprofit and Voluntary Sector Quarterly* 18(4): 367-383.

Lohmann, R. A. 1992. *The Commons: Perspectives on Nonprofit Organization and Voluntary Action.* San Francisco, CA: Jossey-Bass.

COMMENT ON BOETTKE AND PRYCHITKO

Richard Stroup
Montana State University

Boettke and Prychitko undertake a large mission here, especially in the latter portion of their title. In the narrow sense their paper is a critique of the work in this topic area by Lester Salamon, who writes of the failure of the nonprofit sector and calls for more explicit partnerships of nonprofits with government. They make many valid and important points against Salamon's views along the way. He has, it would appear from their critique, failed to show that the sector has failed, and he fails to show that explicit government-nonprofit partnerships would in fact do better. They do make their case on this, bringing in other elements from the literature in doing so. It is a useful paper.

It is in the second, more ambitious part of the mission declared in their title that they fall short. These two leading Austrian economists, both familiar with the Virginia tradition as well, fail to make many points against Salamon, and bypass many points central to the character of the nonprofit sector, that I would expect an Austrian interpretation (especially one with close ties to George Mason University) to bring sharply into focus. They point out, for example, that a vigorous nonprofit sector can fill in and make government unnecessary in the provision of many community services. (They reference Toqueville but fail to provide a citation which would be most welcome here.) Their point is true and important, but they fail to note the critical fact that government provision is different in kind from voluntary assistance and normally brings very different results, many of them unwanted. As Charles Murray and others have shown, for example, when government steps in to provide welfare payments, the result is, in effect, the purchase of more of the behavior leading to the "need" for welfare in the first place.

Volunteer assistance, by contrast, will typically be local and will normally involve "tough love." Family, friends, church members, and others providing nonprofit, voluntary assistance are less likely to tolerate the behaviors that lead to poverty—unwillingness to work, use of drugs, promiscuous behavior leading to unwanted pregnancy, and so on. Such assistance is often explicitly limited to "the deserving" when it is private, unlike government-provided welfare paid by involuntary taxpayers. Such providers of voluntary assistance have local, more intimate knowledge and the tool of shame to work with as well. Government aid is different; it softens the individual's price paid for bad behavior. Bad behavior increases, having in effect been purchased.

The "little platoons" of local clubs, churches, neighborhood groups, and so on, act differently—more holistically, one might say in today's jargon. These groups, described by Murray following Burke's writings much earlier, also form an important part of the social fabric in other areas: once formed to solve one problem, the connections, fellowship, knowledge, and trust gained in one situation are useful in subsequent situations. Individuals understand that joining in is a form of insurance for all. He who does not join in, or who acts in an antisocial manner, will be less well insured. Governmental action tends to displace and destroy the little platoons, making weaker and less resilient the social fabric in the process. Civil society declines, and individual behavior becomes meaner, less civil.

Little platoons of voluntary organizations are different from government in another important way. Government organizations are, we hope, responsive to the electorate in general. A government-supported art gallery must respond to the majority that ultimately rules in a democracy. In a republic, there are mediating forces so that the median voter is not in charge, but still the agency must look to the elected legislature and the elected executives, not primarily to the most passionate gallery-goers. Who pays the piper calls the tune. When taxpayers pay, they have every right to control that for which they pay. "Political interference" is precisely the way the people seek to exercise this right to control their government. If the National Endowment for the Arts is reined in by Senator Jesse Helms for exhibitions of "Piss Christ," it is because Helms' conservative constituents pay the tab, too, just as do the Endowment's biggest liberal backers. Compare that kerfuffle, and its discordant results, with the results of voluntary nonprofit actions. A private art gallery has every right to bring in—or to reject—any artist its governing body chooses. Those unhappy with their decision need not support the gallery in any way.

A characteristic of private property is that neighbors can get along peaceably, each convinced that the other is wrong and may burn in hell later, but neither causing the other any direct harm or expense. For this reason, private philanthropy, characterized by the voluntary giving of time, talent, or money, is categorically a less disruptive approach to social change than are politically mandated transfers.

It is ironic that voluntary action, with its obvious public good "free rider" problem, will often have less of that very problem than government action taken to replace it. Government can levy taxes and solve the financial free-rider problem, but the social costs can be high. At the cost of peace, perhaps, all can be forced to contribute to the National Endowment for (you name it). But who will control the action so financed? It is here that the public sector has a very serious problem. Good government, in the United States at least, means representative democracy. Will the median voter rule? What legislative or executive branch compromises will be reached? As Gordon Tullock pointed out in a no less prominent place than the *Journal of Political Economy* (1971), public decisions truly are public goods, with no clear private responsibility attached to outcomes. Will public schools be run to benefit the children? Who will successfully fight the teachers' unions and the schools of education for control? No one, as it turns out all too often. Who will see that the military, one answer to the greatest of the classic public goods, the defense of the nation, is controlled for the benefit of all, rather than for the benefit of certain suppliers, certain political districts, and so on?

This free rider problem in government is in fact so severe that we may well end up with less, not more, of the supposed good as a result of government subsidy and the resulting political control. A classic case, again from the *Journal of Political Economy* is religion. Two centuries ago, churches in the United States were mostly state supported. (Only later was the Constitution amended so that states, like the federal government, had to live within constitutional limits in this regard.) The argument for state-sponsored religion was that all citizens gained benefits when anyone was more religious—a religious person was thought to be a better citizen, parent, business person, etc. All gained, so all should support the state church. Indeed this idea holds in most industrial democracies today. Yet in the United States, as the states one-by-one disestablished their churches voluntarily, religion blossomed much further. Church attendance rose, financial support increased in total, the number of preachers increased, and so did religiosity. Why? Presumably, churches run by members only, not at the direction of a majority of voters or their elected representatives, are different churches (or synagogues, mosques, etc.), and thus worthy of much more support—and not coincidentally, control—by those most ardent in the faith. To this day, no other industrial democracy is in a class with the United States in the social importance of religion—because of, not despite, the lack of government support for religion.

No one knows better than an Austrian economist that preferences (not to mention passions) are individual and subjective matters, not even objectively measurable. This acknowledgment of goods being different when produced by different groups, is conspicuous by its absence in the paper under review.

If a little platoon, or a big one for that matter, is run by a committee, then very often it will best be run by a committee of those closest to the problem to be solved or the opportunity to be sought after. Closeness may be defined by geographical proximity, or as in many cases, simply a closely aligned set of passions for the action to be taken. Being joined together in a diverse state, much less a nation, is seldom sufficient for such purposes, yet that is where much of government is financed.

Indeed, most cities are far too large and far too diverse for a city government to effectively run a little platoon or any but the most bland of art galleries, much less a church of any kind. Only when nearly everyone in the city can agree on the action to be taken (murder and theft to be stopped, and courts to enforce such criminal laws, for example) is the political process likely to be reasonably effective and with little added rancor. Yet when ethnic neighborhoods are important and standards of proper behavior vary among them, then even criminal law may need some more local control than the city as a whole can provide. It is not just that voluntary action can reduce the need for government, which Boettke and Prychitko properly point out, but also that government simply cannot truly replace much of what voluntary action can and does accomplish. Salomon is not just wrong: his "partnership with government" approach to voluntary action is too often pernicious as well, when the services sought are important. Government is just not capable of accomplishing much of what we might seek from it, especially in the case of local or specialized services.

A crucial part of voluntary action is the joining together of people holding like goals to get the job done. Others, less intensely involved, will properly have little role to play and correspondingly little voice and little burden to bear. Each goal will be better met when those with the greatest desire for successful action, and thus also probably those most knowledgeable in organizing that action, are in charge. Not being a great fan of ballet, I should logically have no say in how it is done. And when it is done voluntarily, I am sure to avoid polluting the wisdom of zealots who know and care about the subject far more than I. But if my tax dollars support the ballet, then I have every right to have the same voice as those who know the topic far better because they care far more than I do. The latter is a sad situation all around.

Boettke and Prychitko seem not to note that problem, yet it is crucial to an understanding of what voluntary action means, why it is important, and why voluntary action is diluted and indeed polluted when financial aid is taken from government. In that situation a "partnership" is inevitable, but it is also destructive. It reduces effective coordination, turns passion from production to conflict, and can badly damage the social fabric. The painful lessons shown us by Charles Murray in his writings on welfare and poverty, and the hopeful lesson of Kelly Olds on the privatization in the United States of religion, should not be lost or forgotten as we try better to understand the importance and proper place of the voluntary nonprofit sector.

REFERENCES

Olds, Kelly. 1994. "Privatizing Religion: Disestablishment in Connecticut and Massachusetts." *The Journal of Political Economy* 102 (2): 277-297.

Murray, Charles. 1984. *Losing Ground: American Social Policy: 1950-1980.* New York: Basic Books.

Tullock, Gordon. 1971. "Public Decisions as Public Goods." *Journal of Political Economy* 79 (4): 913-18.

CONVERSATION 2

The Necessity of Overcoming the Prejudice of Political Philosophy as a Condition for Philanthropy

Steven D. Ealy

WITH COMMENTS BY

Gus DiZerega

Eugene Miller

Gordon Lloyd

Conversations on Philanthropy Volume I: Conceptual Foundations

®*DonorsTrust*
2004

CONTRIBUTORS

GUS DIZEREGA is the author of *Persuasion, Power and Polity: A Theory of Democratic Self-Organization* (2000). He is a leading theorist of evolutionary liberalism, a liberal ethic regrounded in awareness of our relationship with the earth, with all life, and with Spirit and growing in appreciation of how self-organizing systems actually work. He holds a Ph.D. in political science from the University of California at Berkeley and currently teaches in the Department of Government at St. Lawrence University.

STEVEN D. EALY is a Senior Fellow at Liberty Fund, Inc., an Indianapolis-based educational foundation. He previously taught at Western Carolina University and Armstrong Atlantic State University. He has published on Jurgen Habermas, bureaucratic ethics, the Federalist Papers, and Robert Penn Warren.

GORDON LLOYD earned his bachelor's degree in economics and political science at McGill University. He completed all coursework toward a doctorate in economics from the University of Chicago before receiving his master's and Ph.D. degrees in government at Claremont Graduate School. The co-author of three books on the American founding and author of two forthcoming publications on political economy, he also has numerous articles and book reviews to his credit. His areas of research span the California constitution, common law, the New Deal, slavery and the Supreme Court, and the relationship between politics and economics.

EUGENE MILLER is Professor Emeritus of Political Science in the School of Public and International Affairs at the University of Georgia. He has written extensively on the history of political philosophy and American political thought. He approaches issues of philanthrophy in light of his broader interests in moral philosophy, political epistemology, and technology and politics. He is editor of the Liberty Fund edition of David Hume's *Essays Moral, Political, and Literary.*

THE NECESSITY OF OVERCOMING THE PREJUDICE OF POLITICAL PHILOSOPHY AS A CONDITION FOR PHILANTHROPY

Steven D. Ealy

This paper addresses the question, "Why does the political solution to social problems appear to be the default position in contemporary America?" A complete answer to this question would take us to the heart of the dynamic of American society, and would involve considerations of historical development, contemporary politics, and political philosophy. An answer to this question is central to any effort to move away from government and toward independent voluntary action as a means of dealing with social and community problems. An alternative to the default move to government control is crucial if philanthropy is going to have an independent life of its own as opposed to simply being one more piece of equipment in the political toolbox.

A complete answer to the question at hand is not provided here; rather, I deal with one component of the problem. This paper approaches the subject not by examining contemporary attitudes or the immediate historical framework for the development of American philanthropy, but by examining how political philosophy frames our understanding of social life.

In the first section of this paper, I will examine a major premise underlying political philosophy identified by Leo Strauss: the notion that "the political association...is the most comprehensive or authoritative association" in society. I will offer a critique of this position based on the argument that "the political" exists in the modern world only by analogy, and that the use of the political analogy allows many assumptions, perhaps true of the ancient Greek *polis*, to be applied without serious thought to the modern state. In the second section, I argue that this question is of more than historical interest, as an examination of both conservative and liberal arguments will demonstrate.

Ealy, Steven D. 2004. The Necessity of Overcoming the Prejudice of Political Philosophy as a Condition for Philanthropy. *Conversations on Philanthropy I*: 67-84. ISSN 1552-9592 © 2004 DonorsTrust.

The focus of that section will be the arguments made by conservative political commentator George Will in *Statecraft as Soulcraft: What Government Does* and those of William James in "The Moral Equivalent of War." In the final section of this paper I will consider alternatives to the position of preeminence given to the state by all three of these writers.

Among other things, my discussion of Strauss and Will is intended to emphasize the underlying irony of much contemporary political action and debate. Many conservative political writers (including Will himself on occasion) point to "collectivistic liberalism" as the intellectual source for the growth of government. Neither Leo Strauss nor George Will is a part of the liberal establishment, yet their arguments provide a foundation for the development of government as expansive and intrusive as that supported by the left.

I

In an essay entitled "What is Political Philosophy?" Leo Strauss argues that political philosophy as a discipline is committed to an unwavering search for the truth, especially in regard to the question of the good society. But this total dedication to pursuing the truth appears to be challenged by Strauss himself when he contrasts political philosophy with what he identifies as "social philosophy." Strauss writes, "Political philosophy rests on the premise that the political association—one's country or one's nation—is the most comprehensive or the most authoritative association..." (Strauss, 1959, 13).[1] This position presents a number of difficulties to the individual interested in discovering what the "good society" would look like.

A major difficulty with Strauss's view is that his "premise" predetermines the answer to one of the most important questions that must be addressed in uncovering the good society—the question of where ultimate authority should reside. The prejudgment of political philosophy places this authority with or within the political system, but there are at least two alternative views contending against this position.

One view, which holds that there need be no central "comprehensive and authoritative" authority at all, can be further subdivided. The better-known half would be anarchism, which sees no need for social authority at all. Each man, independent and autonomous, should make his own decisions in isolation, and society should leave it to the "invisible hand" to coordinate any spillover benefits or ills to other equally autonomous and independent individuals. But it is possible to oppose the notion of a single authority and still see that (empirically) some authority does seem to rule in most social situations and that (normatively) authority is not per se illegitimate. Authority thus may be free-floating, attached to different institutions at different times and under differing conditions, and variable. We can tentatively identify this view as "polycentricism," which maintains that there are independent sources of authority and judgment that act informally but collectively in determining community standards of behavior and the focus of collective (but voluntary) action. A model for this view is represented by the work of Michael Polanyi on the nature of the scientific community (Polanyi, 1964, 15-17, 42-62).[2]

The other position contending with the Straussian supremacy of politics maintains that some institution or group other than the political is deserving of the privileged position in society. To complete the spectrum of possibilities, we simply need to note that there are other challengers for the title of "most comprehensive and authoritative" institution. Among these challengers would be religious institutions, business and economic concerns, and legal and market mechanisms. Strauss recognizes this challenge to his position—the "social philosophy" he contrasts political philosophy with "conceives of the political association as a part of a larger whole which it designates by the term 'society'" (Strauss, 1959, 13).

A second difficulty presented by the Straussian perspective, although not as obvious as the first merely on the basis of this initial quotation, is the claim that the appropriate model for political action is the classical understanding of politics. That is, the political community is truly "most comprehensive," and not only for external matters (defense and security) but also is the locus of the most important internal matters (education and morality) with which human beings must deal. To use the phrase made popular by pundit George Will, political philosophy (at least the Straussian variety) sees "statecraft as soulcraft." Although American conservatives are often identified as proponents of "limited government," most are proponents of governmental restraints in some areas and governmental activism and expansion in other areas. George Will is a leading spokesman for an activist brand of American conservatism. A current example of conservative expansionism would be the Bush administration's establishment of an office to coordinate volunteerism in American society.

The implication of the Straussian view of politics for an understanding of the proper role of philanthropy is straightforward: if political institutions are both authoritative and concerned with all aspects of human life, all activity— even those actions normally deemed private or charitable—must be subsumed under political review and control. Thus from this perspective, even if the decision was made to allow "private" philanthropic activities to be carried out, they would do so under the guidelines of the comprehensive and deter- mining political agenda. Although progressivism may have set the immediate institutional and historical setting for the development of American philan- thropy, I would argue that a broader intellectual understanding of the status of the political order in human life, one akin to that described by Strauss, underlies the specific details of progressivism.

This understanding of politics, Strauss argues, grew naturally out of the Greek *polis*. Although modern mass industrial society no longer shares the impor- tant characteristics that made the *polis* distinct, we still live in the shadow of the *polis* intellectually. We live in its shadow, first, in that many of the terms still used in political and social discourse had their origins in classical Greek thought. We live in the shadow of the *polis*, second, in that the Greek *polis* is taken by many today to be the model of the healthy and well-functioning society.

One approach to these issues is offered in a closely reasoned essay by the political philosopher Eugene F. Miller, "What Does 'Political' Mean?" (Miller, 1980). After examining the various things to which the word *political* is applied, Miller concludes, "the meaning of 'political' is neither univocal nor empirical" (Miller, 1980, 57). This conclusion leads Miller to a consideration of Aristotle's understanding of univocals and equivocals. Miller explains: "things named univocally have in common both the name and the definition answering to the name; things named equivocally have a name in common, but a different definition" (Miller, 1980, 57). Whereas Aristotle identifies a number of types of equivocals, Miller concerns himself with only two: the *pros hen* type of equivocal and the equivocal based on analogy.

The Greek term *pros* hen literally means "to one" (Miller, 1980, 59). Miller states, "things of this type have the same name because of a common reference or relation to some one thing," and notes that Aristotle's favorite examples of *pros hen* equivocals are "healthy" and "medical" (Miller, 1980, 60). If the word *political* is to be understood as a *pros hen* equivocal, it must have a "focal meaning"; that is, it must have "many senses pointing in many ways to a central sense."[3] So, Miller asks, what is the primary experience to which the word *political* refers? He concludes, "The primary instance of something political, and thus the central or focal meaning of the term, is the political community, the *polis*. Other things are called political by reference to this primary instance" (Miller, 1980, 61).

This *pros hen* understanding allowed Aristotle and his contemporaries to use the term *political* by reference to the Greek *polis*, Miller continues, but this is not an adequate foundation for understanding the modern use of the term, for the *polis* no longer exists.[4] Miller finally concludes that the modern usage of *political* can be salvaged through Aristotle's understanding of analogy: "the state or nation bears an analogical likeness to the *polis*; and the term 'political,' when applied to both, is an equivocal by analogy" (Miller, 1980, 66-67).

For our immediate purposes, the crucial element in Miller's argument is his discussion of the absence of the *polis* from the modern world. "The *polis* has been superseded by the modern 'state' or 'nation', and this type of association is something very different from the *polis*," Miller argues, going so far as to suggest that "a persuasive case can be made that the two are fundamentally opposed" (Miller, 1980, 64).

While some of the differences may appear to be superficial, such as size, the key difference between the *polis* and the state is intellectual. Miller underlines the importance of the different intellectual foundations of *polis* and state by arguing, "The modern vocabulary of politics originates in political theory that specifically opposes the sort of authoritative community that the *polis* represented. The *polis* was understood to aim at the good or happy life for man, and the education of its members in virtue was thought to be required by this aim" (Miller, 1980, 64). Modern society, on the other hand, "is the web or network of human relationships that arise from the striving of individuals to attain their private ends, and the 'state' is the agency that guarantees the means or conditions for this striving. Far from having a comprehensive authority over the life of man, the state has only the authority that is necessary to secure the rights of individuals and the safety of the whole society" (Miller, 1980, 64). Miller concludes this contrast by reiterating the Aristotelian position that the *polis* is the most authoritative community and arguing "it is doubtful if the state can be understood as a species of the genus community at all" (Miller, 1980, 65).

The burden of this paper is to deal with the twin prejudices on the part of political philosophy—that political institutions should be the most authoritative and that the political system has the "regime responsibility" for shaping the moral life of its citizens—and to show that these positions do not fit well with the nature of modern society. Miller's discussion of the differences between the Greek *polis* (the experiential foundation for Greek political philosophy) and the modern state, is a first step in decoupling classical moral and political philosophy from the modern practice of politics, but it is not sufficient.

As Miller's discussion of the meaning of the word *political* suggests, even when we are using that term to describe the modern, mass, democratic, religiously neutral state, the very words we use continue to carry some of the resonance of their earlier application and usage in the ancient, small, and religiously and morally committed communities of Greece. Thus there is a psychology built into the very political language we use that inclines us toward the position articulated by Strauss.

The difficulty in overcoming the "prejudices of political philosophy" can be underlined by noting that the conclusions I draw from Eugene Miller's thoughtful analysis of the word *political* diverge radically from Miller's own conclusion:

> In order to speak intelligibly of political things and to understand them, we are compelled to seek some insight into the nature of the polis as a distinctive kind of human community and into the fundamental differences between the polis and other ways of associating to achieve common purposes. Since this insight is no longer available to us directly from experience, we must turn attentively to the classical writings in political philosophy, whose theme is the polis and its right ordering (Miller, 1980, 72).

From my perspective, a large part of our problem in limiting government to its proper role in social life stems from the political philosophy smuggled into our thinking by the use of an analogical language that keeps pointing us back to ancient Athens and its expansive political institutions. That difficulty will only be intensified if we turn for an understanding and clarification of contemporary political concerns to the very writers whose views have distorted the nature of modern social and political life.

II

Thus far my discussion may perhaps be construed to suggest that these are arcane issues of interest only to a few specialists in ancient Greek thought, but in the remainder of this paper I address the more immediate political relevance of the preceding argument. In 1981, George Will, today known as a conservative newspaper columnist and political commentator on television, delivered the Godkin Lectures at Harvard University, which were published under the title *Statecraft as Soulcraft: What Government Does* (Will, 1983). Will's book can be seen as an extended essay on the conservative understanding of political life, and indeed Will writes in the preface, "My aim is to recast conservatism in a form compatible with the broad popular imperatives of the day"(Will, 1983, 12).

Will begins by referring to an opinion written by Justice Felix Frankfurter. In *West Virginia v. Barnette* Frankfurter wrote, "Law is concerned with external behavior, and not with the inner life of man." While claiming that he does not understand what Frankfurter meant, Will claims to be sure that what Frankfurter said was untrue. He then states forthrightly, "the purpose of this book is to say why that proposition is wrong" (Will, 1983, 20). Let us turn to an examination of the argument Will builds against Frankfurter. It will be obvious, as this discussion proceeds, that Will parallels closely the views of classical political philosophy discussed in the first section of this paper.

What does Will understand the place of politics and the role of government to be? There is, scattered throughout *Statecraft as Soulcraft*, mention of at least five separate (but overlapping and self-reinforcing) functions for the political system. First, and upon which all of the other functions build, is politics' responsibility for the "the steady emancipation of the individual through the education of his passions" (Will, 1983, 27). Will raises a couple of cautions along the way—he says that this is a purpose that politics shares with religion, and one that requires prudence—but ultimately he accepts as legitimate the classical view that political institutions have primary responsibility for moral education.

There is a two-fold argument at the heart of classical political thought that Will also appears to accept: (1) there are natural standards for human conduct—that is, there is a natural standard of excellence; and (2) government's agents are the teachers and enforcers of those natural standards. This discussion recurs when Will talks of "law as tutor" (Will, 1983, 77). Perhaps the strongest statement Will makes in this regard is his claim that "The abandonment of soulcraft was an abandonment of a pursuit of excellence," (Will, 1983, 43) suggesting that there could be no such pursuit outside of politically controlled channels.

The second function to be performed by the political system grows out of the first: the "creation of social cohesion which proceeds from shared adherence to a public philosophy and shared emulation of exemplary behavior and values." Such cohesion is not the result of "spontaneous combustion," Will notes in an oblique critique of the liberal concept of spontaneous order, but instead is a product of actions by the state, or "by statecraft that is soulcraft" (Will, 1983, 55).

A third function of government, according to Will, is to provide the foundations for the production of wealth: "Government produces the infrastructure of society—legal, physical, educational, from highways through skills—that is a precondition for the production of wealth" (Will, 1983, 125). Will argues that conservatives need to adopt "an affirmative doctrine of the welfare state," (Will, 1983, 126) a political arrangement that he argues may be necessary for the full development of human capital. Will extends this creative power of government to include the establishment of economic structures and mechanisms: "a 'free-market' economic system is a system; it is a public product, a creation of government" (Will, 1983, 125). Even more sweeping is Will's conclusion that "any important structure of freedom is a structure, a complicated institutional and cultural context that government must nurture and sustain" (Will, 1983, 123). Will seems incapable of considering the possibility of human creativity apart from governmental encouragement and management.

In a variation on an earlier point, but one important enough to list separately as a fourth function, Will asserts that "the aim of politics...is a warm citizenship, approximating friendship, based on a sense of shared values and a shared fate" (Will, 1983, 142). This "social warmth," or community, "depends, to some extent, on policies which generate the feeling that we are and ought to be in some corporate enterprise that stands for something" (Will, 1983, 143). Note that Will is unclear on how crucial public policy is for promoting "warm citizenship," as well as on exactly what public concerns it is that these policies should be addressing. Will maintains that, because state action has alleviated most of the physical distress we once confronted, we now have "societies in which the most important problems are of the spirit" (Will, 1983, 143). Man has other needs that cannot be reduced to physical or material needs—metaphysical, spiritual, moral, and emotional—and which society cannot afford to ignore. The implication appears to be that state action must now be directed toward the amelioration of man's spiritual, moral, emotional, and metaphysical distress.

Fifth, he says, "an aim of prudent statecraft is to limit the state by delegating many of its chores to intermediary institutions" (Will, 1983, 145). At this point Will acknowledges the potential dangers of government, and the passage is therefore worth quoting at length:

> Government can become, to a dangerous degree, an interest group, as self-interested as any other, and more abusive than most. But government can apply to itself a kind of antitrust policy. With all its dimensions, from law through rhetoric, government can encourage strength in private institutions just as surely as totalitarian regimes work to enfeeble such institutions (Will, 1983, 145).

The key point to note in Will's discussion is the presumption that the right to act resides with the government. While government may choose to delegate some of its "chores" to private institutions, those chores are always the responsibility of government first. Although Will acknowledges the existence of "private institutions" that may be used to achieve governmental objectives, he does not speak of "independent institutions." There seems to be no real sense of the importance of "countervailing power" or alternative, freestanding, private centers of authority that could pursue alternative goals or intervene in the policy process.

Will concludes *Statecraft as Soulcraft* with a paean to politics that is so breathtaking in its sweep and implications that I will quote it without any additional comment:

> Politics involves an endless agenda of arduous choices; it can be thrilling and noble. Certainly a sense of the complexity and majesty of politics is indispensable to the care of our time (Will, 1986, 165).

I have presented, in rough outline form, Will's case against Felix Frankfurter and his argument for why law should be concerned with "the inner life of man." As Will explains it, this concern with the inner life provides the foundation for government—the state—to attend to the most intimate of human relationships and to manipulate the economic system[5] in order to alleviate man's physical and metaphysical distress. The checks on the use of this political power appear to be internal to government itself—self-application of an "antitrust policy," as Will puts it. The presumption throughout this book is that the most important human concerns—the care for excellence, the creative energies of society, and the moral and spiritual vision of a people—are all somehow embodied in and controlled by the political structures of society. Intermediary institutions, the private sector, a relatively free market mechanism, voluntary associations—all of these appear to be of secondary importance, useful at times because government may choose to delegate a few chores to them.

Near the end of *Statecraft as Soulcraft*, Will quotes William James as follows: "Civilization is always in need of being saved. The nation blest above all nations is she in whom the civic genius of the people does the saving day by day . . ." (Will, 1983, 161). I believe that there is a deeper connection between Will's conservative activism and James's progressivism than is generally assumed, and therefore conclude this section with a brief discussion of James's very important essay "The Moral Equivalent of War" (James, 1987). This is a rich essay, deserving of more attention than I will give it here.[6] This brief discussion of James is designed to do two things: to point back toward progressivism as an important foundation for the political and social development of America during the twentieth century, and to show an underlying connection between American liberalism and American conservatism (at least the "conservatism" represented by Will).

The issue James confronts is this: How can the martial virtues, which are both essential to the development of civilization and at the same time a threat to civilization, be maintained and made safe as the world becomes more pacific? James writes,

A permanently successful peace-economy cannot be a simple pleasure-economy. In the more or less socialist future towards which mankind seems drifting we must still subject ourselves collectively to those severities which answer to our real position upon this only partly hospitable globe. We must make new energies and hardihoods continue the manliness to which the military mind so faithfully clings. Martial virtues must be the enduring cement; intrepidity, contempt of softness, surrender of private interest, obedience to command, must still remain the rock upon which states are built (James, 1987, 1289-90).[7]

James's solution to the problem he sets forth is, first, to recognize that the martial virtues are "absolute and permanent human goods" (James, 1987, 1290). Patriotism and military ambition are but variations on man's "general competitive passion." The second step is to transfer these virtues and emotional energies toward some non-militaristic goal. He suggests, for example, "instead of military conscription a conscription of the whole youthful population to form for a certain number of years a part of the army enlisted against *Nature*." (James, 1987, 1291). James envisions armies of American youths working in coal mines, on freight trains, on fishing ships, and in other settings, being disciplined and trained in the way the military forces discipline and train recruits, but toward peaceful and socially productive ends.

But for this vision to come to fruition, James notes, we must approach social problems as the "moral equivalent of war," for without the passions released by war, we will not have the energy or focus to address these challenging but more mundane problems. James writes, "I have no serious doubt that the ordinary prides and shames of social man, once developed to a certain intensity, are capable of organizing such a moral equivalent as I have sketched, or some other just as effective for preserving manliness of type. It is but a question of time, of skillful propagandism, and of opinion-making men seizing historic opportunities" (James, 1987, 1292).

James believes that the martial spirit can be bred and maintained without war, because examples of "strenuous honor and disinterestedness" can be found everywhere. "Priests and medical men are in a fashion educated to it, and we should all feel some degree of it imperative if we were conscious of our work as an obligatory service to the state" (James, 1987, 1292). James continues,

> We should be *owned*, as soldiers are by the army, and our pride would rise accordingly. We could be poor, then, without humiliation, as army officers now are. The only thing needed henceforward is to inflame the civic temper as past history has inflamed the military temper (James, 1987, 1292).

The historical point that should be made is that twentieth century America, in an amazing way, carried out the strategy James outlined in 1910. Think of the various New Deal programs which mobilized hundreds of thousands of Americans toward building or rebuilding the country's infrastructure, the development of the Peace Corps and Vista, the War on Poverty, the War on Illiteracy, the War on Drugs—all of these as a part of the great progressive effort to channel human energies into the "moral equivalents of war."

The political point that I want to make is that there is a connection between James's view that we should see "our work as an obligatory service to the state" and Will's view that "An aim of prudent statecraft is to limit the state by delegating many of its chores to intermediary institutions." In both views the center of power, the creative center, is the state, and the citizenry are properly seen as secondary to, and subjects of, the state. When George Will can write, "My purpose here is only to sample the range of possible uses of assertive government to achieve conservative goals," (Will, 1983, 130) is his world of conservatism really far removed from the liberal or progressive world of William James?

The question to be raised concerning the place of philanthropy in social life, based on either James's or Will's understanding of politics, is simple: is there any place in their society for an independent and vital philanthropic enterprise? The answer in both cases, I believe, is clearly negative. At best, philanthropy might achieve the status of an intermediary institution to which government might delegate a chore or two, but certainly not the status of independent institutions from which alternative visions of the good life could flow and which could legitimately participate in the public life of the community as a proponent of those views. Hence, in the concluding section of this paper I will briefly point to alternative ways of thinking about the relationship between politics and private life that hold out the possibility of a more robust philanthropy.

III

I began with a discussion of Leo Strauss's claim that "the political association...is the most comprehensive or authoritative association in society." I will conclude with a brief discussion of Michael Polanyi and Michael Oakeshott, two twentieth century thinkers who offer alternatives to the political vision of Strauss and Will, and whose views are more compatible with the development of an independent philanthropy.[8]

Michael Polanyi was a successful research chemist whose professional work led him to consider the broader implications of science as an institution; first, to an examination of the nature of the scientific enterprise and questions of scientific governance, and then, to a consideration of the institutional arrangements appropriate for complex societies. In 1948, Polanyi delivered a brief radio address under the title "Planned Science," (Polanyi, 1998, 106-111) in which he described the scientific enterprise and explained why true science is resistant to central planning. In this address, Polanyi searches for a metaphor to describe the scientific enterprise, and he rejects the image of men building a house, with the blueprints as the plan. Science is systematic, he says, but "the nature of scientific systems is more akin to the ordered arrangement of living cells which constitute a polycellular organism" (Polanyi, 1998, 109). Scientists cooperate by adjusting their research to the findings and research of other scientists working in the same field as they pursue their own work, just as in embryonic development healthy cells adjust their growth to that of the surrounding cells.

But this image too proves inadequate. "The actual situation...may perhaps be better captured by using Milton's simile, which likens truth to a shattered statue, with fragments lying widely scattered and hidden in many places. Each scientist on his own initiative pursues independently the task of finding one fragment of the statue and fitting it to those collected by others" (Polanyi, 1998). But Polanyi finds even this to be inadequate, for whereas it will be obvious when the statue is incomplete (setting aside certain contemporary works of art), science always appears to be a complete whole.[9] Polanyi therefore modifies Milton's image by stipulating that the shattered statue always appears to be complete even as new pieces are being added and that its meaning is modified—to the surprise of those watching—with each addition. Polanyi notes that this is crucial in understanding why central planning in science cannot work:

> No committee of scientists, however distinguished, could forecast the further progress of science except for the routine extension of the existing system. No important scientific advance could ever be foretold by such a committee. The problems allocated by it would therefore be of no real scientific value. They would either be devoid of originality, or if, throwing prudence to the winds, the committee once ventured on some really novel proposals, their suggestions would invariably prove impractical. For the points at which the existing system of science can be effectively amended reveal themselves only to the individual investigator. And even he can discover only through a lifelong concentration on one particular aspect of science a small number of practicable and really worth-while problems (Polanyi, 1998, 110).

In a number of studies Polanyi continues his critique of central planning in science and his understanding of the "self government of science." The scientific enterprise, he finds, involves what Polanyi calls "general authority," characterized by rules of art and individual freedom to pursue research, "governed" by a loose set of institutions that publicize and evaluate scientific activity and maintain professional standards (Polanyi, 1957, 57-60, *passim*). He then extends his analysis to consider the cognitive limitations on central planning in complex organizations and societies—some of this work paralleling that of Hayek.[10] Although Polanyi uses the term "polycentric" in a technical sense in his papers, I think it can be helpful to think of that term as applicable to an understanding of society which sees multiple sources and locations of social power, none of which are "comprehensive and authoritative" in a final sense—just as there is no "final authority" in science (except in a very temporary and localized way).

A fruitful avenue for future research would be to relate Polanyi's discussion of the self-government of science to a consideration of civil society. The concept of civil society, so popular right now, can be particularly important only to the extent that it is developed with an understanding that community and intermediary institutions are actually independent, control their own affairs, and have the resources and power to influence the direction(s) of social change (as opposed to being merely "delagatees" of governmental chores).

Michael Oakeshott also is a fruitful source of ideas worthy of further exploration and application in relation to the nature of politics and the foundations of philanthropy. I will discuss briefly two of Oakeshott's concerns that are important for the issues raised in this paper. In his brief essay "The Claims of Politics," Oakeshott provides an understanding of the relation between political institutions and the broader society that is quite different from that of Strauss and Will. Politics, Oakeshott argues, rather than being the central activity of the community, "is a highly specialized and abstracted form of communal activity"; rather than being the heart and soul of the community, "it is conducted on the surface of the life of a society and except on rare occasions makes remarkably small impression below that surface" (Oakeshott, 1993, 93).

What, then, is the function of the political system in the life of society? It is "primarily for the protection and occasional modification of a recognized legal and social order." But political institutions are not the creators of, or creative forces within, that social order: "its end and meaning lie beyond itself in the social whole to which it belongs, a social whole already determined by law and custom and tradition, none of which is the creation of political activity. . . .A political system presupposes a civilization; it has a function to perform in regard to that civilization, but it is a function mainly of protection and to a minor degree of merely mechanical interpretation and expression" (Oakeshott, 1993, 93).[11]

Oakeshott underlines the limited scope of the political system in the total life of civilization with his comment on two of the most important and well-known documents in English history: "Political activity may have given us Magna Carta and the Bill of Rights, but it did not give us the contents of these documents, which came from a stratum of social thought far too deep to be influenced by the actions of politicians" (Oakeshott, 1993, 93).

Oakeshott's understanding of politics and society moves the "creative center" outside of government and into the society at large—the notion of a "creative center" in fact runs counter to the thrust of Oakeshott's understanding of society. There are many sources of creativity and renewal in a society, some running in parallel lines and some running at crosscurrents. This is why Oakeshott maintains, "Each [modern European state] was the outcome of human choices, but none was the product of a design" (Oakeshott, 1975, 185). This same comment could be applied to almost all other human institutions—including those that appear clearly to be the result of a single design.

This leads to a second important notion developed by Oakeshott: the distinction between the "civil association" and the "purposive (or enterprise) association."[12] The civil association is responsible for establishing "noninstrumental rules of conduct"—the law (Oakeshott, 1991, 454). Law is to be "noninstrumental" in the sense that it establishes "the rules of the game" but does not aim at any substantive goals to be achieved. "Enterprise associations," in contrast, are characterized by a commitment to a substantive agenda for action. The law, Oakeshott argues, should be a neutral framework that sets minimal requirements that allow individuals to pursue their own substantive ends, either individually or collectively (through enterprise associations). Whereas there can be only one "civil association" in a community (although it can be divided into different units or branches), there can be multiple enterprise associations (with overlapping memberships) pursuing and promoting various causes and differing visions of the good society. Philanthropic institutions would clearly fall into the category of enterprise associations, and would have the freedom to pursue their goals, as do other such associations (voluntary civic groups, churches, business enterprises, etc.). Of course, one of the major issues confronting modern society is the possible capture of the institutions of civil association by enterprise associations, and the subsequent effort to convert noninstrumental law into substantive laws.

The discussion in this final section of this paper has attempted to show that there do exist important alternatives to the classical model of politics espoused by many on both the right and left, alternatives that have a social depth that many economic models of social action seem to lack. All of the issues dealt with in this paper, however, are preliminary to the task of re-envisioning American philanthropy. Thus the purpose of this paper has been limited to trying to clear away one of the important intellectual roadblocks to the fostering of an independent and robust philanthropic enterprise. Overcoming the common prejudice of political philosophy that holds government to be the most authoritative and creative actor in our social life is a necessary condition for a renewed philanthropy, but in itself it is not a sufficient condition for such renewal.

NOTES

[1] In saying this Strauss is restating the view articulated by Aristotle in *The Politics* 1252a.

[2] Polanyi uses the concept of "polycentricity" throughout the essays in *The Logic of Liberty: Reflections and Rejoinders* (1998) to describe the complexity of some types of problems and the way in which the various components of a problem interface. I am using the term to suggest the notion of multiple *loci* of power within a system, sources that are not reducible to a common source.

[3] G. E. L. Owen, "Logic and Metaphysics in Some Earlier Works of Aristotle," in *Aristotle and Plato in the Mid-Fourth* Century, eds. Owen and During (Gotebog, 1960), p. 189, as quoted in Miller, 1980, p. 61.

[4] "This principle is not sufficient to account for the meaning of the term as we use it today. The reason for its insufficiency is this: the primary instance by reference to which political things originally were named has disappeared as an object of everyday experience. 'Healthy' continues to be a *pros hen* equivocal, because health of the body is something that is as accessible to our experience as it was to that of the ancients. Yet the *polis*, which is the primary instance of

something 'political,' has disappeared from view." (Miller, 1980, p. 63)

5   See Will, 1983, pp.124-125 on the subordination of economics to politics and morality.

6   See, for example, the very perceptive comments on the changing nature of war that forecast the development of the garrison state: "Every up-to-date dictionary should say that 'peace' and 'war' mean the same thing, now *in posse*, now *in actu*. It may even reasonably be said that the intensely sharp competitive *preparation* for war by the nations is *the real war*, permanent, unceasing; and that the battles are only a sort of public verification of the mastery gained during the 'peace'-interval." James, 1989, pp. 1283-84. Emphasis in original. This essay was published in February 1910, long before George Orwell made the same point so dramatically in his novel *1984*.

7   James, 1989, pp. 1289-90. This passage continues: "—unless, indeed, we wish for dangerous reactions against commonwealths fit only for contempt, and liable to invite attack whenever a center of crystallization for military-minded enterprise gets formed anywhere in their neighborhood."

8   This is not to claim that there are not important differences—especially philosophical differences—between the two. (Mitchell, 2001) I have argued throughout this paper that the growth of the state, and the intellectual foundations for such growth, can be found on the right as well as the left. By the same token, some on the left are concerned with limiting the sphere of political action and protecting a sphere for private and civic action free from political control. For a recent example, consider William A. Galston: "There are multiple, independent, sometimes competing sources of authority over our lives, and political authority is not dominant for all purposes under all circumstances. Liberalism accepts the importance of political institutions but refuses to regard them as architectonic." (Galston, 2002, p. 4)

9   Consider in this connection Thomas Kuhn's discussion of "normal science."

10   "The Span of Central Direction," "Profits and Polycentrism," and "Manageability of Social Tasks," in Polanyi, 1998.

11   Consider the parallel argument made by Roger A. Lohmann: "If we look at public programs subsidizing the creation and continued operation of various nonprofit corporations, we will probably conclude that the state creates the commons. It is probably sounder, on the whole, to step back and view the state as arising out of the commons than to see the state as engendering the commons. Certainly, this view point is more accurate in the long-term histo-

ry of civilizations." (Lohmann, 1992, pp. 183-84)

[12] For a thoughtful discussion of the importance of enterprise associations for Oakeshott, and the dangers of confusing enterprise and civil associations, see Boyd, 2002.

REFERENCES

Boyd, Richard. 2002. "Michael Oakeshott on Civility, Civil Society, and Civil Association." Paper presented at the 98th annual meeting of the American Political Science Association. A revised version will appear in *Political Studies* (forthcoming, 2005).

Galston, William A. 2002. *Liberal Pluralism: The Implications of Value Pluralism for Political Theory and Practice*. Cambridge: Cambridge University Press.

James, William. 1987. "The Moral Equivalent of War." In *William James, Writings 1902-1910*. The Library of America.

Lohmann, Roger A. 1992. *The Commons*. San Francisco: Jossey-Bass.

Miller, Eugene. 1980. "What Does 'Political' Mean?" *The Review of Politics* 42: 56-72.

Mitchell, Mark T. 2001. "Michael Polanyi and Michael Oakeshott: Common Ground, Uncommon Foundations." *Tradition & Discovery* 28: 23-34.

Oakeshott, Michael. 1975. *On Human Conduct*. Oxford: Oxford University Press.

Oakeshott, Michael. 1991. "Talking Politics." In *Rationalism in Politics and other essays*. Edited by Timothy Fuller. Indianapolis: Liberty Fund.

Oakeshott, Michael. 1993. "The Claims of Politics." In *Religion, Politics and the Moral Life*. Edited by Timothy Fuller. New Haven: Yale University Press.

Polanyi, Michael. 1964. *Science, Faith and Society*. Chicago: University of Chicago Press.

Polanyi, Michael. 1998. *The Logic of Liberty*. Indianapolis: Liberty Fund.

Strauss, Leo. 1959. *"What is Political Philosophy?"* In *What is Political Philosophy? and Other Studies*. New York: The Free Press.

Will, George. 1983. *Statecraft as Soulcraft: What Government Does*. New York: Simon and Schuster.

COMMENT ON EALY

Gus diZerega
St. Lawrence University

I agree with Steve Ealy's goal of moving "away from government and towards independent voluntary action [for] dealing with social and community problems," and with his belief that philanthropy can be a powerful independent force in meeting this challenge. Political theory plays a central, yet so far not very helpful, role in how we think about these issues. When freed from its appropriation by statists, political theory offers us some insights vital for our task. In particular, I want to rescue the concepts of the "political" and the "public" from their current association with coercive government. Re-examining Aristotle gets us started.

Politics as Persuasion

Aristotle's view of politics included both a focus on the *polis* and a recognition that politics should be rooted in rational persuasion, not force. Only corrupt poleis depend on control over coercive power. A tension thus lies at the heart of Aristotle's theory: legitimate political authority relies on rational agreement, and existing poleis are corrupt, with government rooted in force. Much of his *Politics* was an attempt to bridge this chasm (Aristotle, 1958; diZerega, 2000, 13-51).

Distinguishing Aristotle's conception of politics from more coercive visions recovers the terms *politics* and *public* for our own use. In Aristotle's sense, politics consists of free and equal citizens seeking to discover and serve what is good for their community. The term *public* refers to the kinds of values that apply to such communities. Ealy correctly rejects Eugene Miller's equating of the state or nation with the *polis*, but I think he too quickly abandons the Classical tradition. Politics in Aristotle's sense of rational persuasion regarding public values remains very relevant to our current task.

Like the Greek *polis*, liberal democracies offer their citizens a way to discover and address public values. I use the word *value* to differentiate my point from the economists' term, public goods. Public values are ones that some citizens believe should be manifested in societies as a whole rather than simply at the level of individual action. Sometimes this is because that is the only way they can be made manifest, such as a judicial system and reforms to improve it. In other situations, advocates of particular positions believe that their favored public values are already present but are inadequately manifested. Parks and child-care are examples. Putting the matter this way makes it an open question as to whether coercive political institutions can generally do the best job.

Polanyi and Polycentricity

Ealy perceptively argues that the notion of polycentric institutions is central to an understanding of how philanthropy might become a stronger force in serving community needs. To see why, we must grasp how this concept applies in different contexts. Polanyi identifies different polycentric social orders (Polanyi, 1951, 176-80; 1969, 49-72). The market is a well-known example, so I will briefly look at another such order: science. In science, authority comes from freely arrived upon agreement among scientists that particular hypotheses are worthy of being taken seriously. Over time, the scientific community developed persuasive criteria by which this authority is justified, such as repeatable experiments, rational explanation, mathematical precision, and the capacity to make predictions. How these criteria apply varies from field to field, but evaluations by scientists in neighboring fields play a key role in keeping science a unified body of knowledge (Polanyi, 1962, 216; Ziman, 1978, 134-5). Always approached and never fully attained, the scientific ideal is universal agreement (Ziman, 1978).

Science has it easy. There are no time constraints on when an explanation must be accepted or rejected. Some arguments win acceptance only after their originators die in obscurity, as with Alfred Wegner and continental drift and with Gregor Mendel and genetics (Ziman, 92-4; Hull, 1988, 51-3). Some issues persist for decades with no generally agreed upon explanation, such as cosmology. Science is not bothered.

When we consider authority in human society at large, the institutional landscape becomes very different. Most social issues combine more complex values and empirical claims than do most scientific disputes. Relatively impersonal criteria are more difficult to apply. How long should a patent or copyright last? Is it acceptable to cause the death of a species? Decisions like these require large-scale application if they are to work. Time constraints also play a more prominent role in the public realm. Lack of action can lead to great suffering.

Democracy, Authority, Polycentricity

A central question of political theory is how liberal democracies address such social issues and manifest public values. Liberal democracies cannot be accurately described as hierarchies of coercive power, which is the traditional model of the state. Modern democratic polities are polycentric, manifesting many independent sources of political innovation, evaluation, and action (diZerega, 165-208; Kingdon, 1995). Federalist democratic systems involve yet another polycentric dimension (Ostrom, 1991). The closest approximation of a state in a modern democratic polity is the incumbent administration, but unlike a state it is not sovereign. Only in wartime do democracies act like states (diZerega, 1995). Abandoning the state model, which is derived from coercive power hierarchies, we can usefully conceive democracies in Aristotelian fashion as the outcome of people coming together to develop means by which to address common concerns, including evaluating just how common they are and whether to act on them (diZerega, 2001, 760-3; 1995, 296-7).

Recognizing the need sometimes to act, rational citizens adopt rules requiring less than unanimity to facilitate effective action, knowing that they may occasionally lose in the process. In *Federalist 58*, James Madison explained why:

It has been said that more than a majority ought to have been required for a...decision. That some advantages might have resulted from such a precaution cannot be denied. It might have been an additional shield to some particular interests, and another obstacle to hasty and partial measures. But these considerations are outweighed by the inconveniences...In all cases where justice or the general good might require new laws to be passed, or active measures to be pursued, the fundamental principle of free government would be reversed...[P]ower would be transferred to the minority (Rossiter, 361).

Despite the challenges of majoritarian decision making, the modern democratic-republican ideal has remained, as with Aristotle, agreement, not coercion (diZerega, 2000, 13-51).

From this perspective, many market problems liberals associate with democracies can be considered information problems. Those charged as employees of the political community may take advantage of asymmetrical information and high organizing costs to abuse citizens for their own benefit and that of their allies. Asymmetries in information and organizing costs allow some people to use decision-making processes designed to serve public values to service their private interests instead, at the expense of the public in general. Inherent in any organized response to an issue, this problem is exacerbated in democratic institutions enjoying coercive power because the payoff for making decisions in one's own interests is far greater.

When Madison wrote, and particularly after political parties formed, high organizing costs beyond the local level made it seem that public values had to be addressed more centrally by government. Since then, as we have become ever more intertwined and interdependent as a society, the role of public values has in many ways increased, as F. A. Hayek acknowledged (Hayek, 1976, 7). By default, most citizens continue to assume that these values are most appropriately handled by government, because many other kinds of public values have been.

Nevertheless, our task is not to move from a state-centered to a polycentric polity, because we are already there, even if Strauss, James, and Will haven't figured it out. Rather, we need to strengthen the capacity for public values to be served successfully within civil society rather than by government. One reason for optimism is that information and organizing costs, even for complex public values, have fallen markedly in recent years.

Philanthropy, Public Values, and Government

Today many public values are served by both government and philanthropy, including art museums and libraries, parks and nature preserves, hospitals and clinics, schools and colleges, and housing and aid to the poor. The strongest argument for relying on government to supply these values is that civil society alone is inadequate to do so or applies too many strings. But as readers of this volume know, many costs accompany their governmental provision as well.

Some suggest that pursuing any public values through governmental means is simply a case of "rent seeking." This judgment is often—I think very often—mistaken. Many citizens support government programs without self-interested motives and are active in grassroots philanthropy as well. For example, *Mother Jones*, a left-oriented magazine, published an article about the impact of social spending cuts on poor families (Mencimer, 2003). The magazine later reported that a reader had anonymously donated $8,000 to meet a young woman's tuition needs for a year of college (Backtalk, 2004). As a reader of *Mother Jones*, the philanthropist most likely supported governmental social welfare programs, but when informed of their shortcomings in this particular case, contributed greatly to assist a needy person. *Were organizing and information costs low enough, it is possible that all such needs could be met outside the realm of government.*

How do we facilitate the optimum context for discovering public values and acting to provide them without relying on formally coercive mechanisms which have inherent cost inefficiencies and are prone to capture by corrupt agents, private interests, or fanatics? How do we liberate service to the public from the corruption and abuse that so often accompany formally coercive political action? How do we further empower civil society as an independent social process?

Philanthropy is a central player in the process of effectively serving public values by institutions other than formally coercive ones. Politics in its Aristotelian sense must take place today distributed throughout the political system, and it can succeed without eventuating in governmental action. Just as economists have demonstrated that markets are better than coercive political institutions for discovering and coordinating consumer ends, it is probable that many or most public values can be better discovered and served by philanthropic action rooted in formally voluntary relationships than in those where coercion is formally institutionalized.

The challenge, and it is a big one, is to enable those now originating proposals for government action to find practical nongovernmental alternatives. This would turn advocates of pulic values—or many of them, at least—into supporters of philanthropy and civil society rather than of governmental approaches to the addressing of public values. Many are already well aware of the drawbacks to government provision, but they often see little alternative.

Our attention then turns naturally to evaluation of the barriers to successful voluntary action in support of public values, barriers that often turn those seeking such values toward the pursuit of formally coercive means of attaining their ends.

To give an example from environmentalism, most people who treasure wild nature are not statists. They love wild ecosystems and want some means or other of protecting them. Many nongovernmental strategies, however, are foreclosed by law. For example, neither National Forests nor Bureau of Land Management rangelands allow environmentalists to bid against logging companies and ranchers for control over logging or grazing rights. If they could, energy now employed trying to influence governmental policy would go instead towards bidding to protect natural values. Yet when environmentalists turn to the courts and politicians as the only alternative available to them, they are accused by politically privileged timber companies and ranchers of favoring "big government."

The example of bidding rights indicates that the pursuit of voluntary approaches would not be confined to the nonauthoritarian ("libertarian") right. In my view, many on the left would be more open to this approach than would George Will, followers of Leo Strauss, and others dominating the political right today, which makes Ealy's critique important. Furthermore, freeing the term public would help bridge a semantic divide that does the cause of liberty no good at all.

I do not think that all public values can be provided outside government's framework. But the extent to which they can be so provided is far greater than the extent to which they currently are. Therefore, the answer to Ealy's question of why the governmental (not political) solution to social problems remains the default position is ultimately rooted in two factors. First, the mistaken but unilateral association of the public realm with government leads some to turn only to government to serve public values because it seems the only game in town. It inclines others to deny the reality of public values because of their personal hostility to government. Potential cooperation is nipped in the bud. The second factor is the relatively high organizing costs for supplying public values beyond the most local levels by nongovernmental means. With Ealy, my own work offers a rebuttal to the first of these dimensions, and it goes beyond Ealy in pointing out the importance of the positive work of lowering organizing costs in order to enable polycentric and voluntary philanthropic action to identify and effect public values.

REFERENCES

Aristotle. 1958. *Politics*. Trans. Sir Ernest Barker. London: Oxford University Press.

Backtalk. 2004. *Mother Jones*, 29 (6): 14.

diZerega, Gus. 1995. "Democracies and Peace: The Self-Organizing Foundation for the Democratic Peace." *The Review of Politics*, 57 (2): 279-309.

diZerega, Gus. 2000. *Persuasion, Power and Polity: A Theory of Democratic Self-Organization*, Cresskill, NJ: Hampton Press.

diZerega, Gus. 2001. "Liberalism, Democracy and the State: Reclaiming the Unity of Liberal Politics." *The Review of Politics*, 63 (4): 755-82.

Hayek, F. A. 1976. *Law, Legislation, and Liberty*. Vol. 2: *The Mirage of Social Justice*. Chicago: University of Chicago Press.

Hull, David L. 1988. *Science as a Process: An Evolutionary Account of the Social and Conceptual Development of Science*. Chicago: University of Chicago Press.

Kingdon, John. W. 1995. *Agendas, Alternatives, and Public Policies*. 2nd edition. New York: Longman.

Mencimer, Stephanie. 2003. "Death by a Thousand Cuts." *Mother Jones*, 28 (6).

Ostrom, Vincent. 1991. *The Meaning of American Federalism: Constituting a Self-Governing Society*. San Francisco: Institute for Contemporary Studies.

Polanyi, Michael. 1951. *The Logic of Liberty*, Chicago: University of Chicago Press.

Polanyi, Michael. 1962. *Personal Knowledge: Towards a Post-Critical Philosophy*. Chicago: University of Chicago Press.

Polanyi, Michael. 1969. *Knowing and Being: Essays by Michael Polanyi*, Marjorie Grene, ed. Chicago: University of Chicago Press.

Rossiter, Clinton, ed. 1961. *The Federalist Papers*. New York: Mentor.

Ziman, John. 1978. *Reliable Knowledge: An Explanation of the Grounds for Belief in Science*, Cambridge: Cambridge University Press.

COMMENT ON EALY

Eugene F. Miller
University of Georgia (emeritus)

Steven Ealy's provocative essay addresses core issues of politics and philanthropy and, in doing so, shows that intelligent discussion of these issues
requires close attention to our use of language. In fact, his substantive thesis
revolves around the claim that modern thinking about politics and philanthropy is misguided precisely because of the language in which it is framed: specifically, the language of politics that modernity inherited from the ancient
Greeks. In Ealy's view, this traditional language has a built-in "psychology" or
"resonance" that compels us to think about politics very much along the lines
of the Greek political philosophers—a way of thinking that is both inappropriate and dangerous in a world where the modern state has replaced the ancient
polis. In developing his thesis, Ealy takes note of some of my own reflections
about the analogical uses of political language, but he draws a conclusion from
them that is quite different from the one intended. My remarks will speak to
the linguistic and substantive issues that Ealy raises.

I

Analogies presume a likeness or similarity, but not an identity, between
things with a common name. They can mislead us in either of two ways: by
leading us to presume a greater likeness than actually exists or else by causing
us to overlook crucial differences that prevent the things so named from being
identical. With a view to avoiding both of these errors in political discourse,
my own essay emphasized that while the modern state or nation is like the
ancient *polis* in some respects (both are ways of associating to achieve common purposes), in other respects, it is fundamentally different.

I had recommended an attentive study of the classics not to reinstate the
polis, as Ealy implies, but for the following reasons: first, Greek political philosophy offers the best insight into the nature of the *polis* and thus into ways
in which it is *both like* and *unlike* the kinds of associations that are prevalent
today. This insight permits us to learn from the classics while avoiding possi-

Miller, Eugene F. 2004. Comment on Ealy. *Conversations on Philanthropy I*:
92-100. ISSN 1552-9592 © 2004 DonorsTrust.

ble errors of the kind that trouble Ealy. Second, whatever the historical epoch, the very experience of living in associations formed for common purposes gives rise necessarily to a certain kind of discourse—one that tries to articulate those purposes and deliberates about the best way to attain them. The classical political philosophers adopted this kind of discourse, and their writings instruct us about its contours and implications.

Consider, for example, that the Declaration of Independence speaks of the broad ends for which governments are organized ("safety and happiness"), and that the U. S. Constitution, in its Preamble, specifies various purposes for which the government is established (forming a more perfect union, establishing justice, insuring domestic tranquility, providing for the common defense, promoting the general welfare, and securing the blessings of liberty). Here the imperatives of human association itself, and not the residue of classical philosophy, were moving the authors of these documents to take up very basic questions about the purposes of a comprehensive association and to consider a range of alternative answers. Although moderns can think independently of the classics and, indeed, repudiate their principles, they cannot escape these practical imperatives.

II

The substantive concern that drives Ealy's thinking is the danger that expansive government poses to a sphere of life where individual freedom, privacy, and volunteerism can flourish. Ealy believes, as I do, that this sphere should be very wide. The question is whether its flourishing requires a radical displacement of politics of the kind that Ealy envisions, or whether flourishing is more likely to occur in a well-ordered political community.

III

In part I of his essay, Ealy seems to promise a linguistic solution to the substantive problem of expansive government. He leads us to expect that he will discard the language of politics altogether, since even its analogical meaning "keeps pointing us back to ancient Athens and its expansive political institutions." Yet in part III, where he outlines his substantive argument, Ealy speaks freely of "politics" and "the *political* system," suggesting one of two things: either the intended linguistic purge cannot be carried through, or the word political is now being used in some non-analogical sense that remains unspecified.

Ealy defines his task in part III as one of deciding where "the political system" fits into what he refers to variously as "the community," "civilization," "society at large," and "the civil association." It seems that Ealy, having rejected the political community as the comprehensive association, is attempting to find a substitute. But what exactly is "society" or "the community"? These are exceedingly nebulous terms, and Ealy doesn't provide his readers much help in figuring out to what entities they refer. Is there only one encompassing "community" or "society" for humankind at large, or is there instead a plurality of such associations? Is it even possible to recognize, identify, and demarcate these associations apart from political criteria? When people today use such terms as "the community" or "society at large" to refer to broad and inclusive associations, they typically have in mind such entities as "the United States of America," "Canada," or "Mexico," associations whose very constitution and boundaries are political. Indeed, we recognize and identify these inclusive societies primarily by their political structure—the presence of border guards, police and military, the authoritative reach of their laws, and their self-identification as nations organized politically for common purposes.

"The community" or "society at large," as we know it from our experience, is fundamentally a political entity and the locus of what Locke calls "political power," namely "*a Right* of making Laws with Penalties of Death, and consequently all less Penalties, for the Regulating and Preserving of Property, and of employing the force of the Community, in the Execution of such Laws, and in the defence of the Common-wealth from Foreign Injury, and all this only for the Public Good" (Locke, Second Treatise, § 3).

IV

Ealy would curb expansive government by either effacing "the political" or reducing it to just another competitor for authority in some more comprehensive association, but neither option is viable. Political communities—comprehensive associations with final authority—are givens of our experience, and they are unlikely to disappear. They can be constituted, however, in different ways. Our real choice is between better or worse constitutions, and here the tradition of political philosophy, which Ealy would discard, offers valuable guidance. Constitutions quite favorable to Ealy's objectives—limited government, protection for a private sphere, encouragement for voluntary initiatives—have been inspired by the writings of political philosophers. One need only consider the salutary influence of thinkers such as Locke, Montesquieu, Hume, and Adam Smith on America's founding generation. Recognizing legal and coercive institutions with final authority does not jeopardize the vigorous pursuit of private ends, but rather establishes the conditions under which this pursuit can safely take place. As Locke explains, the rule of law makes possible "a Liberty to follow my own Will in all things, where the Rule prescribes not; and not to be subject to the inconstant, uncertain, unknown, Arbitrary Will of another Man" (Locke, Second Treatise, § 22).

How does Ealy assess Locke and the other philosophers who articulated the principles of modern liberty? It is significant that George Will, in the book that Ealy criticizes, is himself attacking the early modern political philosophers as well as American statesmen such as Madison who adopted their principles. One might presume that Ealy would find common ground with those whom Will attacks, but his blanket rejection of "political philosophy" makes no exception for the early moderns whom the American founders admired.

V

Ealy's broad aim is to nurture the private sphere, but his path—elevating "the community" or "society at large" above "the political"—is fraught with danger. No book does more than Helmut Schoeck's *Envy* to disabuse us of the romantic notion that communities as such are favorable to individual freedom, spontaneity, and voluntary initiatives to benefit others. Quite the opposite is true, if we may credit the extensive anthropological evidence that Schoeck reviews. In most communities that have existed in the world, intense envy is directed at those individuals whose efforts or talents or good fortune allow them to stand out above others; and the ubiquitous fear of a destructive envy, operating through such supposed mechanisms as the "evil eye," acts as an internal check on individuals who might otherwise try to get ahead, or amass wealth, or become innovators or benefactors. Fear of envy gives rise to extreme secretiveness, the concealment of one's private affairs, and the avoidance of intimacy. It sabotages cooperative planning for the future and collective undertakings that might benefit the whole community. Schoeck explains that since envy can vent itself simply by remaining passive, "very often the envious man, while not indeed acting so as to harm another, will not voluntarily do anything out of what is called humanity, a feeling of decency (concepts still incomprehensible to the vast majority in the world), to avert another's harm." He illustrates this by citing Oscar Lewis's study of life in a Mexican village: "In general there is an absence of altruism, generosity, charity, and the spirit of sharing." "Doing favors for others is rare and creates suspicion." "Children are scolded for giving things to their friends or for being trusting and generous in lending articles to persons outside the family" (Schoeck, 57-76, 63-64).

Envy is by no means confined to primitive communities. Tocqueville, in his searching account of modern democracy, identifies "a depraved taste for equality in the human heart that brings the weak to want to draw the strong to their level and that reduces men to preferring equality in servitude to inequality in freedom." Ealy fears that governments will be tempted to engage in "soulcraft," but Tocqueville points out that democratic society itself exercises a kind of tyranny over the individual that "goes straight for the soul." Good laws, while less influential than a nation's mores, can help to curb this envious equality and deflect its intrusion into the human soul. They can also promote a "manly and legitimate passion for equality that incites men to want all to be strong and esteemed"—a way of loving equality that inspires voluntary initiatives to lift up the weak (Tocqueville, 52, 244).

In a similar vein, Madison identifies the "injustice of the laws of the states" as the most alarming "vice" that a new federal constitution should correct. Significantly for our purposes, Madison finds the primary source of this vice in "the people themselves" rather than in the state legislatures. The new government that he proposes is designed specifically to check abuses originating in the states as relatively small communities (Madison, 76-80). Communities as such tend toward injustice. A large and comprehensive community, organized politically, with a government that exercises legal and coercive authority with finality, is the best safeguard of those very liberties that Ealy wants to encourage.

VI

Ealy gives detailed consideration to what *political* means, but little if any to the meaning of his other key term, philanthropy. Both terms are polysemous and of Greek origin. Philanthropy means literally the love of man. In perhaps its earliest surviving usage, the poet Aeschylus applied the term to the protagonist of his tragedy *Prometheus Bound*. Prometheus' *philanthropia*—his love of mankind—has led him to defy Zeus and bestow on the weak race of human beings the gift of fire, along with all the arts. Zeus's agents, Might and Hephaestus, both attribute Prometheus' defiance of Zeus to his man-loving *(philanthropou)* ways (lines 11, 28). For this misdeed the Titan is severely punished by Zeus, who had his own plan for improving the human race. As we see, the first recorded "philanthropist" is someone with a grandiose scheme to benefit humanity through the radical transformation of its material condition. To carry out his plan, he is willing to challenge the existing order of things and even to disregard natural or sacred limits. He prides himself in having a godlike wisdom as regards the good for man, and nothing will deter him from applying it. Prometheus' intent was to improve humankind's condition by giving it the arts and fire, along with what he calls "blind hope"—a precursor perhaps of the belief in the indefinite progress or perfectibility of the human race.

Ealy clearly dislikes progressivism's notion of philanthropy, as it emerged in late-nineteenth century America, but perhaps that notion is closer to the original than is Ealy's own understanding of the philanthropic enterprise. How would Ealy define philanthropy? Does he give it the same meaning as its original Greek application, or an analogous meaning, or a meaning that is different altogether, despite the common name? Is philanthropy a generalized love of man or a regard for particular individuals or groups? Is it rooted in aristocratic liberality? In a thirst for justice? In Christian charity? In natural sentiments such as benevolence or compassion? In the utilitarian calculation that benefiting others is the best way to look out for ourselves? And is philanthropy so obviously a good thing as Ealy presumes? Here one recalls literary depictions, by Dostoevsky and others, of persons with truly nasty dispositions who cannot tolerate the people around them but who profess great love for humanity and put forward grand but quite destructive schemes of reform.

As the idea of philanthropy gained momentum in nineteenth-century America, some important writers, including Thoreau, Melville, and Brownson,[1] called attention to its undesirable features. Later a term ("do-gooders") came into use to disparage philanthropists of the unattractive variety. Nothing intrinsic to the meaning of philanthropy certifies its goodness or makes it a private rather than a civic endeavor. Ealy's essay warns of the dangers to liberty and privacy in the modern world. Are these dangers inherent to politics, as Ealy assumes, or do they result largely from the displacement of prudent statesmanship by reformist impulses and ideas, including the philanthropic impulse? Ealy wishes to protect philanthropy against the spirit of politics, but protecting politics against the spirit of philanthropy may be a task of equal or greater urgency.

VII

Is it possible to give proper weight to politics without jeopardizing the private and voluntary philanthropy that Ealy recommends? In approaching this question, it is worthwhile to ponder this sentence in Adam Smith's *Lectures on Jurisprudence*: "The law hinders the doing injuries to others, but there can be no fixed laws for acts of benevolence" (Smith, 1982, 449). Here Smith is acknowledging the indispensable role of law and government in a political community, but is also taking account of natural limits on their power to require virtue and to suppress vice. To understand his thinking, we must note that although Smith regards both justice and beneficence as virtues, he nonetheless identifies important differences between them. As Smith explains in the *Theory of Moral Sentiments*, justice is a virtue "of which the observance is not left to the freedom of our own wills." Justice may properly "be extorted by force." Smith's reasoning here is that "the violation of justice is injury: it does real and positive hurt to some particular persons, from motives which are naturally disapproved of." Since unjust injury or hurt naturally evokes resentment and retaliation, civil punishments are warranted in dealing with injustice. Beneficence, by contrast, "is always free, it cannot be extorted by force." (Smith, 1976, 156ff.)

As Smith explains, the failure to act beneficently may disappoint someone's expectation of receiving a good, but such inaction "does no positive hurt to anybody." This failure, if excessive, will evoke moral disapprobation and therefore is blameworthy, but it is not a proper object of punishment, at least not by those whose expectations are disappointed. Smith gives the example of a man who "shuts his breast against compassion, and refuses to relieve the misery of his fellow-creatures, when he can with the greatest ease." Everybody would blame such conduct, Smith surmises, but nobody would imagine that those who had reason to expect more kindness "have any right to extort it by force." Smith goes on, however, to add an important qualification to his principle that beneficent action must be free and unforced. Although it would be highly insolent and presumptuous "for equals to use force against one another" to compel beneficent acts, a nation may sometimes, through its laws, impose duties of beneficence upon its citizens. Smith explains:

> The laws of all civilized nations oblige parents to maintain their children, and children to maintain their parents, and impose upon men many other duties of benevolence. The civil magistrate is entrusted with the power not only of preserving the public peace by restraining injustice, but of promoting the prosperity of the commonwealth, by establishing good discipline, and by discouraging every sort of vice and impropriety; he may prescribe rules, therefore, which not only prohibit mutual injuries among fellow-citizens, but command mutual good offices to a certain degree.

Having acknowledged that lawgivers may require certain beneficent actions of the citizenry, and also promote good habits, Smith immediately adds a strong note of caution:

> Of all the duties of the lawgiver, however, this, perhaps, is that which it requires the greatest delicacy and reserve to execute with propriety and judgment. To neglect it altogether exposes the commonwealth to many gross disorders and shocking enormities, and to push it too far is destructive of all liberty, security, and justice.

The emphasis here is on moderation—finding the right mean between excessive legislation and none at all. Lawgivers must keep in mind that beneficence "is less essential to the existence of society than justice." Since "it is the ornament which embellishes, not the foundation which supports the building," imposing it is by no means necessary, although this is sometimes desirable. Clearly Smith wants to preserve a broad sphere of civic life where beneficence, in accordance with its very nature, remains free and unforced, but locating its boundaries is a matter of prudent judgment rather than hard and fast rules. Does Ealy, in speaking of philanthropy, have in mind something akin to Smith's idea of beneficence? How, if at all, would his own thinking about justice and benevolence, and about compulsion and freedom, differ from that of Smith?

Would he be willing, as Smith is, to ground his prescriptions in an account of nature? Addressing these questions might be a fruitful way for Ealy to bring greater clarity to his provocative discussion of politics and philanthropy.

NOTES

[1]   See Henry David Thoreau, *Walden*, Ch. I; Herman Melville, *The Confidence-Man*, Ch. 24; Orestes Brownson, *The Spirit-Rapper: An Autobiography*, Chs. 7, 8, 26.

REFERENCES

Locke, John. 1988. "Of Civil Government," in *Two Treatises of Government*, edited by Peter Laslett. Cambridge: Cambridge University Press.

Madison, James. 1999. "Vices of the Political System of the United States," in *Writings*. Edited by Jack N. Rakove. New York: Library of America.

Schoeck, Helmut. 1987. *Envy: A Theory of Social Behavior*. Indianapolis, IN: Liberty Fund.

Smith, Adam. 1976. *The Theory of Moral Sentiments*. Indianapolis: Liberty Classics.

Smith, Adam. 1982. *Lectures on Jurisprudence*. Reprinted Indianapolis: Liberty Classics.

de Tocqueville, Alexis. 2000. *Democracy in America*. Edited by Harvey C. Mansfield and Delba Winthrop. Chicago: University of Chicago Press.

COMMENT ON EALY

Gordon Lloyd
Pepperdine University

Steve Ealy invites us to reject what he calls "the prejudice of political philosophy." He states his purpose clearly: "The burden of this paper is to deal
with the twin prejudices of political philosophy—that political institutions
should be the most authoritative and that the political system has the...respon-
sibility for shaping the moral life of its citizens—and to show that these positions do not fit well with the nature of modern society." But Ealy's "burden"
is, in fact, more than the effort "to show that these positions do not fit well the
nature of modern society."

The controversial core of Ealy's paper is his claim that these twin positions
are (1) actually prejudicial to the very philanthropic enterprise per se and (2)
that the Progressives' project and that of political philosophy are much closer
than we have heretofore appreciated. Put differently, Ealy's claim is that the
alternative to the Progressive, statist agenda is not to be found in political philosophy, because political philosophy is the problem rather than the solution.

I agree with Ealy's proposal: we need a critique of what political philosophy has to offer concerning the necessary and sufficient conditions for the
pursuit of liberty, responsibility, and happiness in the contemporary world.
First, we need to realize that we are actually living in the modern world and
not some ancient fantasyland, nor, I would add, in some futuristic utopia. We
need a modern solution for the problems of modernity, rather than a premodern, or again I would add, a postmodern alternative. Second, we both agree
that political philosophy, to the extent that it does indeed approach coherence
and relevance, is generally antagonistic toward the modern project, especially the claim that limited, decentralized government and an independent private sphere are more conducive to human liberty, communal responsibility,
and personal happiness.

Ealy's central figure is Leo Strauss, a German émigré who has had an
enormous impact on both political philosophy and contemporary American
conservatism. Ealy is particularly concerned about the Straussian "prejudice"
that gives a privileged position to the Aristotelian concept that "the political
solution to social problems appears to be the default position in contemporary

America," and that perhaps America—these are my words, not Ealy's—is ill-founded because no provision was made at the creation of the Constitution for the cultivation of public virtue. Ealy's case against political philosophy is this: (1) Political philosophy is essentially Straussian political philosophy, and it is grounded in the ancient world and puts the *polis* first, and (2) the influential conservative commentator George Will, in arguing that statecraft is soulcraft, relies on the Straussian and the ancients' claim that the political association is authoritative.

Why are these twin positions prejudicial in the modern world? Because, says Ealy, "we still live in the shadow of the *polis* intellectually...[T]he Greek *polis* is taken by many today to be the model of the healthy and well-functioning society." Will's "five functions of the political system" provide a paean to politics. Will's government will concern itself with the "inner life of man," Moreover, says Ealy's Will, "the aim of politics...is a warm citizenship, approximating friendship, based on a sense of shared values and a shared fate." The secondary institutions are precisely that, and they are useful only if and when government should decide to delegate chores from time to time. In other words, neither Strauss nor Will sees a place "in their society for an independent and vital philanthropic enterprise," because they see the paramount importance of the *polis* and believe that the task of the *polis* is the moral education of the citizenry.

But here comes the really controversial part: isn't such a twin prejudice, challenges Ealy, identical to putting "the amelioration of man's spiritual, moral, emotional, and metaphysical distress," in the direct hands of the state? Isn't there an important connection between Will's "breathtaking" appeal to the centrality of the political association and the Progressive William James's 1910 appeal to the "martial virtues" that would "inflame the civic temper" in a moral equivalent of war against whatever terrible social ills had infected America? Ealy thus portrays the Progressive left as being in the same family tree of political philosophy as the Straussian branch of the contemporary Conservative right. Ealy's point is this: there is an important "underlying connection between modern American liberalism and American conservatism (at least the 'conservatism' represented by Will." And they both are connected to the foundational claims of political philosophy, the prejudice of which is articulated by Leo Strauss.

Now this claim by Ealy challenges the well-known antagonism of the

Straussians toward the Progressives. Let me express a certain initial skepticism concerning this challenge. The Progressives aren't interested in the idea of statesmanship because they are not essentially moved by "doing the best with what one has," a hallmark of Aristotelian politics. Nor are they particularly interested in promoting citizenship; for the Progressives, politics is far too complicated to be left to the ordinary citizen working through the rough and tumble of the deliberative process. Politics, in fact, is dirty rather than enriching, as far as the Progressives are concerned, and what they advocate is the replacement of partisan politics with the science of administration, under the guidance of experts, rather than with the art of the statesman. One last note of caution about drawing too close a connection between political philosophy and Progressivism: the ancients genuinely endorsed generosity to others as a personal virtue; the Progressives view philanthropy as a public obligation.

Ealy concludes with a discussion of Michael Polanyi and Michael Oakeshott—and by implication Hayek—all of whom he contrasts with Strauss, Will, and James. According to Ealy, the former challenge the idea that the political association is the most comprehensive and authoritative association and thus provide a view "more compatible with the development of an independent philanthropy." Polanyi rejects the metaphor of the scientific enterprise as men building a house from blueprints. Life, instead, he claims, is "polycentric." Oakeshott argues that rather than being a central activity, politics "is a highly specialized and abstracted form of communal activity." He suggests that "the political system has a limited importance." Accordingly, Oakeshott moves the "creative center" outside of government and posits, instead, the existence of multiple creative centers within society. And, quite correctly, Ealy sees this shift as "a necessary condition for a renewed philanthropy, but in itself it is not a sufficient condition for such renewal." And thus ends this challenging essay.

Ealy concentrates on the critique of modernity from the right, or premodern perspective, and virtually ignores the left, members of which I think are just as prejudiced against the modern project. There is, for example, a widespread left-inspired criticism of classical political philosophy in general, and of Strauss in particular, within the very field of political philosophy itself. Put differently, Strauss and political philosophy are not synonymous. There is, in fact, within contemporary political philosophy a fundamental antagonism toward both Strauss and limited government and the private sector, which exceeds anything that can be attributed to Strauss and his followers.

To be sure, both Strauss and his critics emphasize the vices of modernity, and they both express an embarrassment—a critical component of prejudice—with respect to the modern project. From Hegel to Heidegger, by way of Marx and Nietzsche, the emphasis is on what is wrong—banal, unheroic, mediocre, and self-indulgent—with modernity and why we need a non-modern solution to the problems of modernity. There is indeed something that political philosophers, both left and right, abhor about what Ealy correctly identifies as the hallmarks of modernity: the economic market system and limited political government. Political philosophy, for the most part, impeaches modernity, but I would suggest that ancient, premodern political philosophy is perhaps more compatible with modernity than is the postmodern alternative, if for no other reason than that the ancients recognized the existence of metaphysical foundations. Postmodernists suggest that only power matters, and thus that personal philanthropy is simply another form of the exercise of individual power.

Let me put Ealy's thesis in my own terms: We know that modernity has its faults, but we need to do the best we can with what we have. And modernity is what we have, and philanthropy is what we can do to improve the human condition consistent with an adherence to limited government and free markets. But how do we know this will work out? Ealy emphasizes the necessity of the doctrine of spontaneous order, and I suggest the sufficiency of the concept of self-interest rightly understood. Ealy is surely correct to say that Polyani, Oakeshott, and Hayek identify the necessary condition for a robust private philanthropy; I would add that Tocqueville points out the sufficient condition.

We need to build on Ealy's call that we, in effect, shift from *public policy* to *private action*. But we need then to move forward and make the case for *public action* on the foundation of *private action*. I don't think that Polanyi, Oakeshott, and Hayek have a definitive answer to the important question here: How do you know that spontaneous action produces better and more orderly outcomes? Why is this not, ultimately, also a "prejudice?" Are we not, if we don't take the next step, replacing "the prejudice of political philosophy"—seeing the state or *polis* as the most authoritative actor in our social life—with "the prejudice of the market," the notion that the market ought to be the authoritative source for the distribution of values?

Is conscious *public action* possible, or are we left with the alternatives of *public policy*, endorsed by political philosophy, or *private action*, endorsed by the spontaneous market? Why be privately philanthropic under either the authoritative or the spontaneous model? If the political philosophy model treats economics as subservient to politics, the market model suggests just the reverse. If political philosophers err in identifying spontaneity with anarchy, then market supporters err in identifying statesmanship with coercion. Is there, possibly, a third way?

I think we need a Tocquevellian, modern *public action* solution for the problems of modernity, one that retains spontaneous human initiative and yet appeals to the civic dimension of human existence. One that overcomes the ancient appeal to communal duty without relying exclusively on the invisible hand of the marketplace. As I read Tocqueville, he warns that reliance on ancient sacrifice is inappropriate. But he also warns that the market system may well encourage self-interest wrongly understood: the notion that I help others by helping myself. Tocqueville is arguing for self-interest rightly understood: By helping others, I help myself. In short, that is the case for being privately philanthropic in the modern world.

As Tocqueville said, self-interest rightly understood is not "a sublime doctrine," one that is among the highest of individual virtues. But it is reliable; it brings out the best in modern man; it produces "orderly, temperate, moderate, careful, and self-controlled citizens." Most importantly, it provides an alternative to both the paternalistic state and the market state. It does not encourage an attachment to the prejudice of political philosophy, nor does it encourage us to abandon the fact that we are, by nature, at least partly political animals. The doctrine that "virtue is useful" leads humans "to help one another and disposes them freely to part of their time and wealth for the good of the state." And when we support this practical approach with the dissemination of the "sublime utterance" of Christianity—"we must do good to our fellows for love of God"—we have, in effect, provided the second dimension of the sufficient condition for personal philanthropy that is absent in both the classical model and the market alternative.

DonorsTrust
BUILDING A LEGACY OF LIBERTY

The Project for New Philanthropy Studies is supported by DonorsTrust, the only community-style foundation committed to promoting a free society as instituted in America's founding documents. The Trust holds over $25 million in charitable assets dedicated to supporting causes and public policies that promote limited government, free enterprise, and personal responsibility.

DonorsTrust offers a portfolio of charitable vehicles to individuals and organizations to encourage philanthropy and individual giving as an answer to society's most pervasive and radical needs. As a rule, participants support charitable causes that seek to maximize individual and economic liberty by minimizing government intervention in the personal and public lives of individuals.

The most popular and flexible charitable vehicle offered by the Trust is the donor-advised account. Providing superior tax treatment without the time and expense of a private foundation, the donor-advised account streamlines annual charitable gifts and allows investment in specific philanthropic interests. Account holders may arrange to engage advisors, consultants, or nonprofit organizations to assist with establishing objectives, commissioning research, or overseeing projects.

The most focused and efficient vehicle in the DonorsTrust portfolio is the field of interest fund, which allows individuals, foundations, or corporations to make contributions to a specific area and transfer the responsibility of disbursing grants to DonorsTrust. Contributors are often invited to recommend projects or organizations and are kept abreast of grantmaking activities. Established field of interest funds include Arts and Culture, Economics, Education, Environment, Foreign Relations, Global Liberty, Health, and Social Welfare.

For more information about the advantages of adding any of these charitable vehicles to your personal investment portfolio, contact DonorsTrust at 703.535.3563 or www.donorstrust.org.

111 North Henry Street · Alexandria, VA 22314 · 703.535.3563
www.donorstrust.org